Solaris™ Multithreaded Programming Guide

A Sun Microsystems, Inc. Business

≡

10 9 8 7 6 5 4 3 2 1

0-13-160896-7

SunSoft Press
A Prentice Hall Title

Contents

Multithreaded Programming Guide

Figures

Multithreaded Programming Guide

Tables

Multithreaded Programming Guide

Code Samples

Acknowledgments

Thanks to Gwen Leister, who developed and produced the original documentation version of this book; to Dan Stein, who provided engineering information and also reviewed the manual for technical content; to Chris Prael for his work on the original documentation version of this book; to Professor Tom Doeppner, who provided material for inclusion in this book; and to Astrid M. Julienne for producing the retail version of this book.

Preface

The *Multithreaded Programming Guide* describes the multithreaded programming interfaces for the Solaris™ 2.4 system. This guide shows application programmers how to create new multithreaded programs and how to add multithreading to existing programs.

To understand this guide, a reader must be familiar with

- A UNIX® SVR4 system – preferably the Solaris 2.4 system
- The C programming language – multithreading is implemented through the `libthread` library

How This Guide Is Organized

Chapter 1, "Covering Multithreading Basics," gives a structural overview of the Solaris threads implementation.

Chapter 2, "Programming with Threads," discusses the general threads library routines.

Chapter 3, "Programming with Synchronization Objects," covers the threads library synchronization routines.

Chapter 4, "Programming with the Operating System," discusses changes to the operating system to support multithreading.

Chapter 5, "Safe and Unsafe Interfaces," covers multithreading safety issues.

Chapter 6, "Compiling and Debugging," covers the basics of compiling and debugging.

Chapter 7, "Programming Guidelines," discusses issues that affect programmers writing multithreaded applications.

Appendix A, "Sample Application Code," provides code examples you can refer to for clarification and practice.

Appendix B, "MT Safety Levels: Library Interfaces," is a table listing routines that are safe to use in multithreaded programs.

What Typographic Changes and Symbols Mean

Table PR-1 describes the type changes and symbols used in this guide.

Table PR-1 Typographic Conventions

Typeface or Symbol	Meaning	Example
AaBbCc123	Commands, files, directories, and C functions; code examples	The fork1() function is new. Use ls -a to list all files.
AaBbCc123	Variables, titles, and emphasized words	The *stack_size* value is set by... You *must* specify a zero value.
AaBbCc123	What you type, contrasted with on-screen computer output	system% **cc prog.c**
page(#)	The man page name and section in the *Solaris Reference Manual*	See thr_create(3T).

Sections of program code in the main text are enclosed in boxes:

```
nt test (100);

main()
{
    register int a, b, c, d, e, f;

    test(a) = b & test(c & 0x1) & test(d & 0x1);
```

Covering Multithreading Basics 1

The word *multithreading* can be translated as *many threads of control*. While a traditional UNIX process always has contained and still does contain a single thread of control, multithreading (MT) separates a process into many execution threads, each of which runs independently.

Read this chapter to understand the multithreading basics.

Because each thread runs independently, multithreading your code can:

- Improve application responsiveness
- Use multiprocessors more efficiently
- Improve your program structure
- Use fewer system resources
- Improve performance

1

Defining Multithreading Terms

The following terms are used in this chapter to describe multithreading concepts.

Thread	A sequence of instructions executed within the context of a process
Single-threaded	Restricting access to a single thread
Multithreaded	Allowing access to two or more threads
User-level or Application-level threads	Threads managed by the threads library routines in user (as opposed to kernel) space
Lightweight processes	Threads in the kernel that execute kernel code and system calls (also called LWPs)
Bound threads	Threads that are permanently bound to LWPs
Unbound threads	Threads that attach and detach from among the LWP pool
Counting semaphore	A memory-based synchronization mechanism

Defining Concurrency and Parallelism

Concurrency exists when at least two threads are *in progress* at the same time. Parallelism arises when at least two threads are *executing* simultaneously.

In a multithreaded process on a single processor, the processor can switch execution resources between threads, resulting in concurrent execution. In the same multithreaded process on a shared-memory multiprocessor, each thread in the process can run on a separate processor at the same time, resulting in parallel execution.

When the process has as many threads as, or fewer threads than, there are processors, the threads support system and the operating system ensure that each thread runs on a different processor. For example, in a matrix multiplication with m processors and m threads, each thread computes a row of the result.

Benefiting From Multithreading

Improve Application Responsiveness

Any program in which many activities are not dependent upon each other can be redesigned so that each activity is fired off as a thread. For example, a GUI in which you are performing one activity while starting up another will show improved performance when implemented with threads.

Use Multiprocessors Efficiently

Typically, applications that express concurrency requirements with threads need not take into account the number of available processors. The performance of the application improves transparently with additional processors.

Numerical algorithms and applications with a high degree of parallelism, such as matrix multiplications, can run much faster when implemented with threads on a multiprocessor.

Improve Program Structure

Many programs are more efficiently structured as multiple independent or semi-independent units of execution instead of as a single, monolithic thread. Multithreaded programs can be more adaptive to variations in user demands than are single threaded programs.

Use Fewer System Resources

Programs that use two or more processes that access common data through shared memory are applying more than one thread of control. However, each process has a full address space and operating systems state. The cost of creating and maintaining this large amount of state makes each process much more expensive than a thread in both time and space. In addition, the inherent separation between processes can require a major effort by the programmer to communicate between the threads in different processes or to synchronize their actions.

Combine Threads and RPC

By combining threads and a remote procedure call (RPC) package, you can exploit non-shared-memory multiprocessors (such as a collection of workstations). This combination distributes your application relatively easily and treats the collection of workstations as a multiprocessor.

For example, one thread might create child threads. Each of these children could then place a remote procedure call, invoking a procedure on another workstation. Although the original thread has merely created a number of threads that are now running in parallel, this parallelism involves other computers.

Improve Performance

The performance numbers in this section were obtained on a SPARCstation™ 2 (Sun 4/75). The measurements were made using the built-in microsecond resolution timer.

Thread Creation Time

Table 1-1 shows the time consumed to create a thread using a default stack that is cached by the threads package. The measured time includes only the actual creation time. It does not include the time for the initial context switch to the thread. The ratio column gives the ratio of the creation time in that row to the creation time in the previous row.

These data show that threads are inexpensive. The operation of creating a new process is over 30 times as expensive as creating an unbound thread, and about 5 times the cost of creating a bound thread consisting of both a thread and an LWP.

Table 1-1   Thread Creation Times

Operation	Microseconds	Ratio
Create unbound thread	52	-
Create bound thread	350	6.7
`fork()`	1700	32.7

Thread Synchronization Times

Table 1-2 shows the time it takes for two threads to synchronize with each other using two p and v semaphores.

Table 1-2   Thread Synchronization Times

Operation	Microseconds	Ratio
Unbound thread	66	-
Bound thread	390	5.9
Between processes	200	3

Looking At Multithreading Structure

Traditional UNIX already supports the concept of threads—each process contains a single thread, so programming with multiple processes is programming with multiple threads. But a process is also an address space, and creating a process involves creating a new address space.

Because of this, creating a process is expensive, while creating a thread within an existing process is cheap. The time it takes to create a thread is on the order of a thousand times less than the time it takes to create a process, partly because switching between threads does not involve switching between address spaces.

Communicating between the threads of one process is simple because the threads share everything—address space, in particular. So, data produced by one thread is immediately available to all the other threads.

The interface to multithreading support is through a subroutine library, `libthread`. Multithreading provides flexibility by decoupling kernel-level and user-level resources.

User-level Threads[1]

Threads are visible only from within the process, where they share all process resources like address space, open files, and so on. The following state is unique to each thread.

- Thread ID
- Register state (including PC and stack pointer)
- Stack
- Signal mask
- Priority
- Thread-private storage

Because threads share the process instructions and most of its data, a change in shared data by one thread can be seen by the other threads in the process. When a thread needs to interact with other threads in the same process, it can do so without involving the operating system.

Threads are the primary programming interface in multithreaded programming. User-level threads are handled in user space and so can avoid kernel context switching penalties. An application can have thousands of threads and still not consume many kernel resources. How many kernel resources the application uses is largely determined by the application.

---

1. User-level threads are so named to distinguish them from kernel-level threads, which are the concern of systems programmers, only. Because this book is for application programmers, kernel-level threads are not discussed here.

By default, threads are very lightweight. But, to get more control over a thread (for instance, to control scheduling policy more), the application can bind the thread. When an application binds threads to execution resources, the threads become kernel resources (see "Bound Threads" on page 8 for more information).

To summarize, Solaris user-level threads are:

- Inexpensive to create because they are bits of virtual memory that are allocated from your address space at run time

- Fast to synchronize because synchronization is done at the application level, not at the kernel level

- Easily managed by the threads library, `libthread`

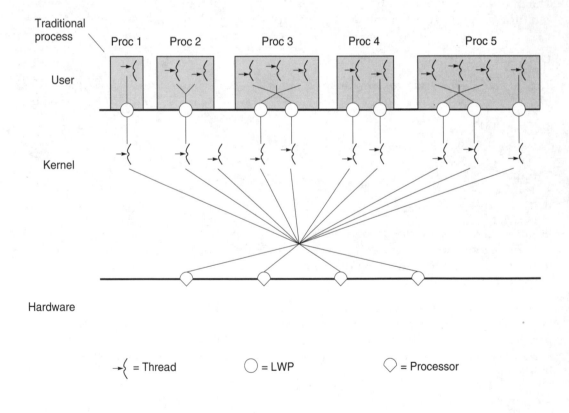

Figure 1-1   Multithreaded System Architecture

Lightweight Processes

The threads library uses underlying threads of control called *lightweight processes* that are supported by the kernel. You can think of an LWP as a virtual CPU that executes code or system calls.

Most programmers use threads without thinking about LWPs. All the information here about LWPs is provided so you can understand the differences between bound and unbound threads, described on page 8.

Note – The LWPs in Solaris 2.x are *not* the same as the LWPs in the SunOS™ 4.0 LWP library, which are not supported in Solaris 2.x.

Much as the `stdio` library routines such as `fopen`(3S) and `fread`(3S) use the `open`(2) and `read`(2) functions, the thread interface uses the LWP interface, and for many of the same reasons.

Lightweight processes (LWPs) bridge the user level and the kernel level. Each process contains one or more LWPs, each of which runs one or more user threads. The creation of a thread usually involves just the creation of some user context, but not the creation of an LWP.

The user-level threads library, with help from the programmer and the operating system, ensures that the number of LWPs available is adequate for the currently active user-level threads. However, there is no one-to-one mapping between user threads and LWPs, and user-level threads can freely migrate from one LWP to another.

The programmer can tell the threads library how many threads should be "running" at the same time. For example, if the programmer says that up to three threads should run at the same time, then at least three LWPs should be available. If there are three available processors, the threads run in parallel. If there is only one processor, then the operating system multiplexes the three LWPs on that one processor. If all the LWPs block, the threads library adds another LWP to the pool.

When a user thread blocks due to synchronization, its LWP transfers to another runnable thread. This transfer is done with a co-routine linkage and not with a system call.

The operating system decides which LWP should run on which processor and when. It has no knowledge about what user threads are or how many are active in each process. The kernel schedules LWPs onto CPU resources according to their scheduling classes and priorities. The threads library schedules threads on the process pool of LWPs in much the same way. Each LWP is independently dispatched by the kernel, performs independent system calls, incurs independent page faults, and runs in parallel on a multiprocessor system.

An LWP has some capabilities that are not exported directly to threads, such as a special scheduling class.

Unbound Threads

Threads that are scheduled on the LWP pool are called unbound threads. You will usually want your threads to be unbound, allowing them to float among the LWPs.

The library invokes LWPs as needed and assigns them to execute runnable threads. The LWP assumes the state of the thread and executes its instructions. If the thread becomes blocked on a synchronization mechanism, or if another thread should be run, the thread state is saved in process memory and the threads library assigns another thread to the LWP to run.

Bound Threads

If needed, you can permanently bind a thread to an LWP.

For example, you can bind a thread to:

- Have the thread scheduled globally (such as realtime)
- Give the thread an alternate signal stack
- Give the thread a unique alarm or timer

Sometimes having more threads than LWPs, as can happen with unbound threads, is a disadvantage.

For example, a parallel array computation divides the rows of its arrays among different threads. If there is one LWP for each processor, but multiple threads for each LWP, each processor spends time switching between threads. In this case, it is better to have one thread for each LWP, divide the rows among a smaller number of threads, and reduce the number of thread switches.

A mixture of threads that are permanently bound to LWPs and unbound threads is also appropriate for some applications.

An example of this is a realtime application that wants some threads to have system-wide priority and realtime scheduling, while other threads attend to background computations. Another example is a window system with unbound threads for most operations and a mouse serviced by a high-priority, bound, realtime thread.

When a user-level thread issues a system call, the LWP running the thread calls into the kernel and remains attached to the thread at least until the system call completes.

Meeting Multithreading Standards

The history of multithreaded programming goes back to at least the 1960s. Its development on UNIX systems goes back to the mid-1980s. Perhaps surprisingly, there is fair agreement about the features necessary to support multithreaded programming. Even so, several different thread packages are available today, each with a different interface.

However, for several years a group known as POSIX 1003.4a has been working on a standard for multithreaded programming. When the standard is finalized, most vendors of systems supporting multithreaded programming will support the POSIX interface. This will have the important benefit of allowing multithreaded programs to be portable.

There are no fundamental differences between Solaris threads and POSIX 1003.4a. Certainly the interfaces differ, but there is nothing that is expressible with one interface that cannot be expressed relatively easily with the other. There are no incompatibilities between the two, so, at least on Solaris systems, there will be one underlying implementation with two interfaces. Even within a single application, you will be able to use both interfaces.

Another reason for using Solaris threads is the collection of support tools supplied with it, such as the multithreaded debugger. `truss`, which traces a program's system calls and signals, has been extended to report on the activities of a program's threads as well.

≡ 1

Programming with Threads

The Threads Library

User-level multithreading is implemented through the threads library, `libthread` (see section 3T in the *man Pages(3): Library Routines*). The threads library supports signals, schedules runnable entities, and handles multiple tasks simultaneously.

This chapter discusses some of the general `libthread` routines, starting with the basic ways to create threads and becoming more advanced.

Create a Thread – the Basics

The thr_create(3T) routine is the most elaborate of all the threads library routines. The explanations in this section are for those cases when you can use the default values for the thr_create() arguments.

More advanced thr_create() use, including explanations of non-default argument values, is covered toward the end of this chapter in "Create a Thread – Advanced Features" on page 26.

thr_create(3T)

Use thr_create() to add a new thread of control to the current process. Note that the new thread does not inherit pending signals, but is does inherit priority and signal masks.

```
#include <thread.h>

int thr_create(void *stack_base, size_t stack_size,
    void * (*start_routine) (void *), void *arg, long flags,
    thread_t *new_thread);

size_t thr_min_stack(void);
```

stack_base – Contains the address for the stack that the new thread uses. If *stack_base* is NULL then thr_create() allocates a stack for the new thread with at least *stack_size* bytes.

stack_size – Contains the size, in number of bytes, for the stack that the new thread uses. If *stack_size* is zero, a default size is used. In most cases, a zero value works best.

There is no general need to allocate stack space for threads. The threads library allocates one megabyte of virtual memory for each thread's stack with no swap space reserved. (The library uses the MAP_NORESERVE option of mmap(2) to make the allocations.)

start_routine – Contains the function with which the new thread begins execution. If *start_routine* returns, the thread exits with the exit status set to the value returned by *start_routine* (see thr_exit(3T)).

flags – Specifies attributes for the created thread. In most cases a zero value works best.

The value in *flags* is constructed from the bitwise inclusive OR of the following. (The last four flags are explained more fully in "Create a Thread – Advanced Features" on page 26.)

THR_DETACHED – Detaches the new thread so that its thread ID and other resources can by reused as soon as the thread terminates. Set this when you do not want to wait for the thread to terminate.

When there is no explicit synchronization to prevent it, an unsuspended, detached thread can die and have its thread ID reassigned to another new thread before its creator returns from `thr_create()`.

THR_SUSPENDED – Suspends the new thread and does not execute *start_routine* until the thread is started by `thr_continue()`.

THR_BOUND – Permanently binds the new thread to an LWP (the new thread is a *bound thread*).

THR_NEW_LWP – Increases the concurrency level for unbound threads by one.

THR_DAEMON   Marks the new thread as a daemon.

new_thread – Points to a location (when *new_thread* is not NULL) where the ID of the new thread is stored. In most cases a zero value works best.

Return Values — `thr_create()` returns a zero and exits when it completes successfully. Any other returned value indicates that an error occurred. When any of the following conditions are detected, `thr_create()` fails and returns the corresponding value:

EAGAIN   A system limit is exceeded, such as when too many LWPs have been created.

ENOMEM   Not enough memory was available to create the new thread.

EINVAL   *stack_base* is not NULL and *stack_size* is less than the value returned by `thr_min_stack()`.

Get the Thread Identifier

thr_self(3T)

Use `thr_self(3T)` to get the ID of the calling thread.

```
#include <thread.h>

thread_t thr_self(void)
```

Return Values — `thr_self()` returns the ID of the calling thread.

Yield Thread Execution

thr_yield(3T)

`thr_yield()` causes the current thread to yield its execution in favor of another thread with the same or greater priority.

```
#include <thread.h>

void thr_yield(void);
```

Suspend or Continue Thread Execution

thr_suspend(3T)

`thr_suspend()` suspends thread execution.

```
#include <thread.h>

int thr_suspend(thread_t target_thread);
```

`thr_suspend()` immediately suspends the execution of the thread specified by *target_thread*. On successful return from `thr_suspend()`, the suspended thread is no longer executing. Once a thread is suspended, subsequent calls to `thr_suspend()` have no effect.

Return Values — thr_suspend() returns zero after completing successfully. Any other returned value indicates that an error occurred. When the following condition occurs, thr_suspend() fails and returns the corresponding value:

ESRCH   *target_thread* cannot be found in the current process.

thr_continue(3T)

thr_continue() resumes the execution of a suspended thread. Once a suspended thread is continued, subsequent calls to thr_continue() have no effect.

```
#include <thread.h>

int thr_continue(thread_t target_thread);
```

A suspended thread will not be awakened by a signal. The signal stays pending until the execution of the thread is resumed by thr_continue().

Return Values — thr_continue() returns zero after completing successfully. Any other returned value indicates that an error occurred. When the following condition occurs, thr_continue() fails and returns the corresponding value:

ESRCH   *target_thread* cannot be found in the current process.

Send a Signal to a Thread

thr_kill(3T)

thr_kill() sends a signal to a thread.

```
#include <thread.h>
#include <signal.h>

int thr_kill(thread_t target_thread, int sig);
```

thr_kill() sends the signal *sig* to the thread specified by *target_thread*. *target_thread* must be a thread within the same process as the calling thread. The *sig* argument must be from the list given in signal(5).

When *sig* is zero, error checking is performed but no signal is actually sent. This can be used to check the validity of *target_thread*.

Return Values — thr_kill() returns zero after completing successfully. Any other returned value indicates that an error occurred. When any of the following conditions occur, thr_kill() fails and returns the corresponding value:

EINVAL   *sig* is not a valid signal number.

ESRCH   *target_thread* cannot be found in the current process.

Access the Signal Mask of the Calling Thread

thr_sigsetmask(3T)

Use thr_sigsetmask() to change or examine the signal mask of the calling thread.

```
#include <thread.h>
#include <signal.h>

int thr_sigsetmask(int how, const sigset_t *set, sigset_t *oset);
```

The *how* argument determines how the signal set is changed and can have one of the following values:

SIG_BLOCK – Add *set* to the current signal mask, where *set* indicates the set of signals to block.

SIG_UNBLOCK – Delete *set* from the current signal mask, where *set* indicates the set of signals to unblock.

SIG_SETMASK – Replace the current signal mask with *set*, where *set* indicates the new signal mask.

When the value of *set* is NULL, the value of *how* is not significant and the signal mask of the thread is unchanged. So, to inquire about currently blocked signals, assign a NULL value to the *set* argument.

When the *oset* argument is not NULL, it points to the space where the previous signal mask is stored.

Return Values — thr_sigsetmask() returns a zero when it completes successfully. Any other returned value indicates that an error occurred. When any of the following conditions are detected, thr_sigsetmask() fails and returns the corresponding value:

EINVAL   The value of *set* is not NULL and the value of *how* is not defined.

EFAULT   Either *set* or *oset* is not a valid address.

Terminate a Thread

thr_exit(3T)

Use thr_exit() to terminate a thread.

```
#include <thread.h>

void thr_exit(void *status);
```

The thr_exit() function terminates the calling thread. All thread-specific data bindings are released. If the calling thread is not detached, then the thread's ID and the exit status specified by *status* are retained until the thread is waited for. Otherwise, *status* is ignored and the thread's ID can be reclaimed immediately.

Return Values — When the calling thread is the last non-daemon thread in the process, the process terminates with a status of zero. When the initial thread returns from main() the process exits with a status equal to the return value.

Finishing Up

A thread can terminate its execution in two ways. The first is simply to return from its first (outermost) procedure. The second is to call thr_exit(), supplying an exit code. What happens next depends upon how the *flags* parameter was set when the thread was created.

The default behavior of a thread (which happens when the appropriate bit in the *flags* parameter is left as zero) is to remain until some other thread has acknowledged its demise by "joining" with it. The result of the join is that the joining thread picks up the exit code of the dying thread and the dying thread vanishes. You can set a bit in the *flags* parameter, by ORing into it THR_DETACHED, to make the thread disappear immediately after it calls thr_exit() or after it returns from its first procedure. In this case, the exit code is not picked up by any thread.

An important special case arises when the main thread, the one that existed initially, returns from the main procedure or calls exit(). This action causes the entire process to be terminated, along with all its threads. So take care to ensure that the main thread does not return from main prematurely.

Note that when the main thread merely calls thr_exit(), it terminates only itself—the other threads in the process, as well as the process, continue to exist. (The process terminates when all threads terminate.)

Note also that if a thread is nondetached, then it is very important that some thread join with it after it terminates—otherwise the resources of that thread are not released for use by new threads. So when you do not want a thread to be joined, create it as a detached thread.

An additional *flags* argument to thr_create() is THR_DAEMON. Threads created with this flag, daemon threads, are automatically terminated when all non-daemon threads have terminated. These daemon threads are especially useful within libraries.

Daemon threads can be created within library routines—as daemon threads they are effectively invisible to the rest of the program. When all other threads in the program (the threads you were aware of creating) terminate, these daemon threads automatically terminate. If they were not daemon threads, they would not terminate when the other threads do, and the process would not exit.

Wait for Thread Termination

thr_join(3T)

Use the thr_join() function to wait for a thread to terminate.

```
#include <thread.h>

int thr_join(thread_t wait_for, thread_t *departed,
    void **status);
```

The thr_join() function blocks the calling thread until the thread specified by *wait_for* terminates. The specified thread must be in the current process and must not be detached. When *wait_for* is (thread_t)0, then thr_join() waits for any undetached thread in the process to terminate. In other words, when no thread identifier is specified, any undetached thread that exits causes thr_join() to return.

When *departed* is not NULL, it points to a location that is set to the ID of the terminated thread when thr_join() returns successfully. When *status* is not NULL, it points to a location that is set to the exit status of the terminated thread when thr_join() returns successfully.

When a stack was specified when the thread was created, the stack can be reclaimed when thr_join() returns. The thread identifier returned by a successful thr_join() can then be used by thr_create().

Multiple threads cannot wait for the same thread to terminate. If they try to, one thread returns successfully and the others fail with an error of ESRCH.

Return Values — thr_join() returns a zero when it completes successfully. Any other returned value indicates that an error occurred. When any of the following conditions are detected, thr_join() fails and returns the corresponding value:

ESRCH   *wait_for* is not a valid, undetached thread in the current process.

EDEADLK   *wait_for* specifies the calling thread.

Final Steps

The thr_join() routine takes three arguments, giving you some flexibility in its use. When you want the caller to wait until a specific (nondetached) thread terminates, supply that thread's ID as the first argument. When you want the caller to wait until any nondetached thread terminates, supply a zero for the first argument.

When the caller wants to find out who the terminated thread is, the second argument should be the address of storage into which the defunct thread's ID will be placed.

Otherwise, supply a zero for this argument. Finally, if you are interested in the exit code of the defunct thread, supply the address of an area to receive it.

A thread can wait until all non-daemon threads have terminated by executing the following:
```
  while(thr_join(0, 0, 0) == 0)
    ;
```

The declaration for the third parameter of thr_join(), void **, might look strange. The corresponding argument of thr_exit() is *void *. The intent is that you pass an arbitrary 4-byte item as the exit code. The C for "arbitrary 4-byte argument" cannot be void, because that means that there is no argument. So it is void *. Because the third parameter of thr_join() is an output parameter that must point to whatever is supplied by thr_exit(), its type is necessarily void **.

Remember that thr_join() works only for target threads that are nondetached. When there is no reason to synchronize with the termination of a particular thread, then that thread should be detached.

Think of a detached thread as being the usual sort of thread and reserve nondetached threads for only those situations that require them.

A Simple Threads Example

In Code Example 2-1 on page 20, one thread executes the procedure at the top, creating a helper thread that executes the procedure `fetch`, which involves a complicated database lookup and might take a while. The mainline thread wants the results of the lookup but has other work to do in the meantime. So it does those other things and then waits for its helper to complete its job by executing `thr_join()`.

The result is passed as a stack parameter, which can be done here because the main thread waits for the spun-off thread to terminate. In general, though, it is better to `malloc(3C)` storage from the heap instead of passing an address to thread stack storage.

Code Example 2-1   A Simple Threads Program

```
void mainline (...) {
        char int result;
        thread_t helper;
        int status;


        thr_create(0,0, fetch, &result,0, &helper);

            /* do something else for a while */

        thr_join(helper, 0, &status);
        /* it's now safe to use result */
    }


    void fetch(int *result) {

            /* fetch value from a database */

        *result = value;
        thr_exit(0);


    }
```

Maintain Thread-Specific Data

Single-threaded C programs have two basic classes of data—local data and global data. For multithreaded C programs a third class is added—thread-specific data (TSD). This is very much like global data, except that it is private to a thread.

Thread-specific data is maintained on a per-thread basis. TSD is the only way to define and refer to data that is private to a thread. Each thread-specific data item is associated with a key that is global to all threads in the process. Using the key, a thread can access a pointer (void *) that is maintained per-thread.

Maintain thread-specific data with the following three functions.

- thr_keycreate() – Create a key specific to the process threads.
- thr_setspecific() – Bind a thread value to the key.
- thr_getspecific() – Store the value in a specific location.

thr_keycreate(3T)

thr_keycreate() allocates a key that is used to identify thread-specific data in a process. The key is global to all threads in the process, and all threads initially have the value NULL associated with the key when it is created.

Once a key has been created, each thread can bind a value to the key. The values are specific to the binding thread and are maintained for each thread independently.

```
#include <thread.h>

int thr_keycreate(thread_key_t *keyp,
  void (*destructor) (void *value));
```

When thr_keycreate() returns successfully, the allocated key is stored in the location pointed to by *keyp*. The caller must ensure that the storage and access to this key are properly synchronized.

An optional destructor function, *destructor*, can be associated with each key. When a key has a non-NULL destructor function and the thread has a non-NULL value associated with that key, the destructor function is called with the current associated value when the thread exits. The order in which the destructor functions are called for all the allocated keys is unspecified.

Return Values — thr_keycreate() returns zero after completing successfully. Any other returned value indicates that an error occurred. When any of the following conditions occur, thr_keycreate() fails and returns the corresponding value:

EAGAIN   The key name space is exhausted.

ENOMEM   Not enough memory is available.

thr_setspecific(3T)

```
#include <thread.h>

int thr_setspecific(thread_key_t key, void *value);
```

thr_setspecific() binds *value* to the thread-specific data key, *key,* for the calling thread.

Return Values — thr_setspecific() returns zero after completing successfully. Any other returned value indicates that an error occurred. When any of the conditionsbelow occur, thr_setspecific() fails and returns the corresponding value:

ENOMEM   Not enough memory is available.

EINVAL   *key* is invalid.

thr_getspecific(3T)

```
#include <thread.h>

int thr_getspecific(thread_key_t key, void **valuep);
```

thr_getspecific() stores the current value bound to *key* for the calling thread into the location pointed to by *valuep*.

Return Values — thr_getspecific() returns zero after completing successfully. Any other returned value indicates that an error occurred. When the following condition occurs, thr_getspecific() fails and returns the corresponding value:

EINVAL   *key* is invalid.

Global and Private Thread-Specific Data

Code Example 2-2 shows an excerpt from a multithreaded program. This code is executed by any number of threads, but it has references to two global variables, errno and mywindow, that really should be references to items private to each thread.

Code Example 2-2   Thread-Specific Data – Global but Private

```
body() {
    ...

    while (write(fd, buffer, size) == -1) {
        if (errno != EINTR) {
            fprintf(mywindow, "%s\n", strerror(errno));
            exit(1);
        }
    }

    ...

}
```

References to errno should get the system error code from the system call called by this thread, not by some other thread. So, references to errno by one thread refer to a different storage location than references to errno by other threads.

The mywindow variable is intended to refer to a stdio stream connected to a window that is private to the referring thread. So, as with errno, references to mywindow by one thread should refer to a different storage location (and, ultimately, a different window) than references to mywindow by other threads. The only difference here is that the threads library takes care of errno, but the programmer must somehow make this work for mywindow.

The next example shows how the references to mywindow work. The preprocessor converts references to mywindow into invocations of the _mywindow procedure.

This routine in turn invokes `thr_getspecific()`, passing it the `mywindow_key` global variable (it really is a global variable) and an output parameter, `win`, which receives the identity of this thread's window.

Code Example 2-3   Turning Global References Into Private References

```
#define mywindow _mywindow()

thread_key_t mywindow_key;

FILE *_mywindow(void) {
    FILE *win;

    thr_getspecific(mywindow_key, &win);
    return(win);
}


void thread_start(...) {
    ...
    make_mywindow();
    ...
}
```

The `mywindow_key` variable identifies a class of variables for which each thread has its own private copy; that is, these variables are thread-specific data. Each thread calls `make_mywindow()` to initialize its window and to arrange for its instance of `mywindow` to refer to it.

Once this routine is called, the thread can safely refer to `mywindow` and, after `_mywindow`, the thread gets the reference to its private window. So, references to `mywindow` behave as if they were direct references to data private to the thread.

Code Example 2-4 shows how to set this up.

Code Example 2-4   Initializing the Thread-Specific Data

```
void make_mywindow(void) {
    FILE **win;
    static int once = 0;
    static mutex_t lock;

    mutex_lock(&lock);
    if (!once) {
        once = 1;
        thr_keycreate(&mywindow_key, free_key);
    }
    mutex_unlock(&lock);

    win = malloc(sizeof(*win));
    create_window(win, ...);

    thr_setspecific(mywindow_key, win);
}

void free_key(void *win) {
    free(win);
}
```

First, get a unique value for the key, mywindow_key. This key is used to identify the thread-specific class of data. So, the first thread to call make_mywindow calls thr_keycreate(), which assigns to its first argument a unique key. The second argument is a destructor function that is used to deallocate a thread's instance of this thread-specific data item once the thread terminates.

The next step is to allocate the storage for the caller's instance of this thread-specific data item. Having allocated the storage, a call is made to the create_window routine, which somehow sets up a window for the thread and sets the storage pointed to by win to refer to it. Finally, a call is made to thr_setspecific(), which associates the value contained in win (that is, the location of the storage containing the reference to the window) with the key.

After this, whenever this thread calls thr_getspecific(), passing the global key, it gets the value that was associated with this key by this thread when it called thr_setspecific().

When a thread terminates, calls are made to the destructor functions that were set up in thr_keycreate(). Each destructor function is called only if the terminating thread established a value for the key by calling thr_setspecific().

Create a Thread – Advanced Features

thr_create(3T)

```
#include <thread.h>

int thr_create(void *stack_base, size_t stack_size,
    void *(*start_routine) (void *), void *arg, long flags,
    thread_t *new_thread);

size_t thr_min_stack(void);
```

stack_base—Contains the address for the stack that the new thread uses. When *stack_base* is NULL then thr_create() allocates a stack for the new thread with at least *stack_size* bytes.

stack_size—Contains the size, in number of bytes, for the stack that the new thread uses. If *stack_size* is zero, a default size is used. If *stack_size* is not zero, it must be greater than the value returned by thr_min_stack().

A stack of minimum size might not accommodate the stack frame for *start_routine*, so if a stack size is specified it must provide for the minimum requirement plus room for the *start_routine* requirements and for the functions that *start_routine* calls.

Typically, thread stacks allocated by thr_create() begin on page boundaries and any specified size is rounded up to the next page boundary. A page with no access permission is appended to the top of the stack so that most stack overflows result in sending a SIGSEGV signal to the offending thread. Thread stacks allocated by the caller are used as is.

When the caller passes in a pre-allocated stack, that stack cannot be freed until the thr_join() call for that thread has returned, even when the thread is known to have exited. Then the process exits with a status equal to the return value.

Generally, you do not need to allocate stack space for threads. The threads library allocates one megabyte of virtual memory for each thread's stack with no swap space reserved. (The library uses the MAP_NORESERVE option of mmap(2) to make the allocations.)

Each thread stack created by the threads library has a red zone. The library creates the red zone by appending a page to the top of a stack to catch stack overflows. This page is invalid and causes a memory fault if it is accessed. Red zones are appended to all automatically allocated stacks whether the size is specified by the application or the default size is used.

Specify stacks or their sizes to thr_create() only when you're absolutely certain you know that they are correct. There are very few occasions when it is sensible to specify a stack, its size, or both to thr_create(). It is difficult even for an expert to know if the right size was specified. This is because even an ABI-compliant program can't determine its stack size statically. Its size is dependent on the needs of the particular runtime environment in which it executes.

Building Your Own Stack

When you specify the size of a thread stack, be sure to account for the allocations needed by the invoked function and by each function called. The accounting should include calling sequence needs, local variables, and information structures.

Occasionally you want a stack that is a bit different from the default stack. An obvious situation is when the thread needs more than one megabyte of stack space. A less obvious situation is when the default stack is too large. You might be creating thousands of threads and just not have the virtual memory necessary to handle the several gigabytes of stack space that this many default stacks require.

The limits on the maximum size of a stack are often obvious, but what about the limits on its minimum size? There must be enough stack space to handle all of the stack frames that are pushed onto the stack, along with their local variables and so on.

You can get the absolute minimum on stack size by calling thr_min_stack(), which returns the amount of stack space required for a thread that executes a null procedure. Useful threads need more than this, so be very careful when reducing the stack size.

You can specify a custom stack in two ways. The first is to supply a NULL for the stack location, thereby asking the runtime library to allocate the space for the stack, but to supply the desired size in the stack-size parameter to thr_create().

The other approach is to take overall aspects of stack management and supply a pointer to the stack to thr_create(). This means that you are responsible not only for stack allocation but also for stack deallocation—when the thread terminates, you must arrange for the disposal of its stack.

When you allocate your own stack, be sure to append a red zone to its end by calling mprotect(2).

start_routine – Contains the function with which the new thread begins execution. When *start_routine* returns, the thread exits with the exit status set to the value returned by *start_routine* (see thr_exit(3T)).

Note that you can supply only one argument. To get your procedure to take multiple arguments, encode them as one (such as by putting them in a structure). This argument can be anything that is described by void, which is typically any 4-byte value. Anything larger must be passed indirectly by having the argument point to it.

flags – Specifies attributes for the created thread. In most cases you want to supply a zero to the *flags* argument.

The value in *flags* is constructed from the bitwise inclusive OR of the following.

THR_SUSPENDED – Suspends the new thread and does not execute *start_routine* until the thread is started by thr_continue(). Use this to operate on the thread (such as changing its priority) before you run it. The termination of a detached thread is ignored.

THR_DETACHED – Detaches the new thread so that its thread ID and   other resources can by reused as soon as the thread terminates. Set this when you do not want to wait for the thread to terminate.

When there is no explicit synchronization to prevent it, an unsuspended, detached thread can die and have its thread ID reassigned to another new thread before its creator returns from thr_create().

THR_BOUND – Permanently binds the new thread to an LWP (the new thread is a *bound thread*).

THR_NEW_LWP – Increases the concurrency level for unbound threads by one. The effect is similar to incrementing concurrency by one with thr_setconcurrency(3T), although this does not affect the level set through the thr_setconcurrency() function. Typically, THR_NEW_LWP adds a new LWP to the pool of LWPs running unbound threads.

When you specify both THR_BOUND and THR_NEW_LWP, two LWPs are typically created—one for the bound thread and another for the pool of LWPs running unbound threads.

THR_DAEMON – Marks the new thread as a daemon. The process exits when all non-daemon threads exit. Daemon threads do not affect the process exit status and are ignored when counting the number of thread exits.

A process can exit either by calling exit(2) or by having every thread in the process that was not created with the THR_DAEMON flag call thr_exit(3T). An application, or a library it calls, can create one or more threads that should be ignored (not counted) in the decision of whether to exit. The THR_DAEMON flag identifies threads that are not counted in the process exit criterion.

new_thread – Points to a location (when *new_thread* is not NULL) where the ID of the new thread is stored when thr_create() is successful. The caller is responsible for supplying the storage this argument points to. The ID is valid only within the calling process.

If you are not interested in this identifier, supply a zero value to *new_thread*.

Return Values — thr_create() returns a zero and exits when it completes successfully. Any other returned value indicates that an error occurred. When any of the following conditions are detected, thr_create() fails and returns the corresponding value:

EAGAIN   A system limit is exceeded, such as when too many LWPs have been created.

ENOMEM   Not enough memory was available to create the new thread.

EINVAL   *stack_base* is not NULL and *stack_size* is less than the value returned by thr_min_stack().

thr_create(3T) Example

Code Example 2-5 on page 30 shows how to create a default thread with a new signal mask (new_mask) that is assumed to have a different value than the creator's signal mask (orig_mask).

In the example, new_mask is set to block all signals except for SIGINT. Then the creator's signal mask is changed so that the new thread inherits a different mask, and is restored to its original value after thr_create() returns.

This example assumes that SIGINT is also unmasked in the creator. When it is masked by the creator, then unmasking the signal opens the creator up to this signal. The other alternative is to have the new thread set its own signal mask in its start routine.

Code Example 2-5   thr_create() Creates Thread With New Signal Mask

```
thread_t tid;
sigset_t new_mask, orig_mask;
int error;

(void)sigfillset(&new_mask);
(void)sigdelset(&new_mask, SIGINT); (void)thr_sigsetmask(SIGSETMASK,
&new_mask, &orig_mask):
error = thr_create(NULL, 0, dofunc, NULL, 0, &tid);
(void)thr_sigsetmask(SIGSETMASK, NULL, &orig_mask);
```

Get the Minimal Stack Size

thr_min_stack(3T)

Use thr_min_stack(3T) to get the minimum stack size for a thread.

```
#include <thread.h>

size_t thr_min_stack(void);
```

thr_min_stack() returns the amount of space needed to execute a null thread (a null thread is a thread that is created to execute a null procedure).

A thread that does more than execute a null procedure should allocate a stack size greater than the size of thr_min_stack().

When a thread is created with a user-supplied stack, the user must reserve enough space to run the thread. In a dynamically linked execution environment, it is difficult to know what the thread minimal stack requirements are.

Most users should not create threads with user-supplied stacks. User-supplied stacks exist only to support applications wanting complete control over their execution environments.

Instead, users should let the threads library manage stack allocation. The threads library provides default stacks that should meet the requirements of any created thread.

Get and Set Thread Concurrency Level

thr_getconcurrency(3T)

Use `thr_getconcurrency()` to get the current value of the desired concurrency level. Note that the actual number of simultaneously active threads can be larger or smaller than this number.

```
#include <thread.h>

int thr_getconcurrency(void)
```

Return Values — `thr_getconcurrency()` always returns the current value for the desired concurrency level.

thr_setconcurrency(3T)

Use `thr_setconcurrency()` to set the desired concurrency level.

```
#include <thread.h>

int thr_setconcurrency(new_level)
```

Unbound threads in a process might or might not be required to be simultaneously active. To conserve system resources, the threads system ensures by default that enough threads are active for the process to make progress and to ensure that the process will not deadlock through a lack of concurrency.

Because this might not produce the most effective level of concurrency, `thr_setconcurrency ()` permits the application to give the threads system a hint, specified by *new_level*, for the desired level of concurrency.

The actual number of simultaneously active threads can be larger or smaller than *new_level*.

Note that an application with multiple compute-bound threads can fail to schedule all the runnable threads if `thr_setconcurrency()` has not been called to adjust the level of execution resources.

You can also affect the value for the desired concurrency level by setting the `THR_NEW_LWP` flag in `thr_create()`.

Return Values — thr_setconcurrency() returns a zero when it completes successfully. Any other returned value indicates that an error occurred. When any of the following conditions are detected, thr_setconcurrency() fails and returns the corresponding value:

EAGAIN   The specified concurrency level would cause a system resource to be exceeded.

EINVAL   The value for *new_level* is negative.

Get and Set Thread Priority

An unbound thread is usually scheduled only with respect to other threads in the process using simple priority levels with no adjustments and no kernel involvement. Its system priority is usually uniform and is inherited from the creating process.

thr_getprio(3T)

Use thr_getprio() to get the current priority for the thread.

```
#include <thread.h>

int thr_getprio(thread_t target_thread, int *pri)
```

Each thread inherits a priority from its creator. thr_getprio() stores the current priority, *target_thread*, in the location pointed to by *pri*.

Return Values — thr_getprio() returns zero after completing successfully. Any other returned value indicates that an error occurred. When the following condition occurs, thr_getprio() fails and returns the corresponding value:

ESRCH   *target_thread* cannot be found in the current process.

thr_setprio(3T)

Use thr_setprio() to change the priority of the thread.

```
#include <thread.h>

int thr_setprio(thread_t target_thread, int pri)
```

`thr_setprio()` changes the priority of the thread, specified by *target_thread*, within the current process to the priority specified by *pri*. By default, threads are scheduled based on fixed priorities that range from zero, the least significant, to the largest integer. The *target_thread* will preempt lower priority threads, and will yield to higher priority threads.

Return Values — `thr_setprio()` returns zero after completing successfully. Any other returned value indicates that an error occurred. When any of the following conditions occur, `thr_setprio()` fails and returns the corresponding value:

ESRCH   *target_thread* cannot be found in the current process.

EINVAL   The value of *pri* makes no sense for the scheduling class associated with the *target_thread*.

Scheduling and the Threads Library

The following `libthread` routines affect thread scheduling.

- `thr_setprio()` and `thr_getprio()`
  These routines alter and retrieve the priority of the *target_thread*, which is the priority used by the scheduler in the user-level threads library, and not the priority used by the operating system to schedule LWPs.

  This priority affects the assignment of threads to LWPs—when there are more runnable threads than there are LWPs, the higher-priority threads are given LWPs. The scheduling of threads is preemptive, meaning that when a thread becomes runnable and its priority is higher than that of some thread currently assigned to an LWP, and there are no other available LWPs, then the lower-priority thread must relinquish its LWP to the higher-priority thread.

- `thr_suspend()` and `thr_continue()`
  These routines control whether a thread is allowed to run. By calling `thr_suspend()`, you put a thread into the suspended state, meaning that it is set aside and will not be granted an LWP even if one is available. The thread is taken out of this state when some other thread calls `thr_continue()` with the suspended thread as the target. These two routines should be used with care—their effects can be dangerous. For example, the thread being suspended might be holding a lock on a mutex, and suspending it could result in a deadlock.

  A thread can be created in the suspended state by including the THR_SUSPENDED flag in the flags parameter of `thr_create()`.

- `thr_yield()`

  The `thr_yield()` routine causes the calling thread to relinquish its LWP when a thread of equal priority is runnable and not suspended. (There cannot be a runnable thread of higher priority that is not running, since it would have taken the LWP by preemption.) This routine is of particular importance because there is no time-slicing of threads on LWPs (although, of course, the operating system time-slices the execution of LWPs).

Finally, note that `priocntl(2)` also affects thread scheduling. See "LWPs and Scheduling Classes" on page 76 for more information.

Programming with
Synchronization Objects 3 ≡

This chapter describes the four synchronization types available with threads and discusses synchronization concerns.

Synchronization objects are variables in memory that you access just like data. Threads in different processes can synchronize with each other through synchronization variables placed in shared memory, even though the threads in different processes are generally invisible to each other.

Synchronization variables can also be placed in files and can have lifetimes beyond that of the creating process.

The types of synchronization objects are:

- Mutex Locks
- Condition Variables
- Readers/Writer Locks
- Semaphores

Here are some multithreading situations in which synchronization is important.

- Threads in two or more processes can use a single synchronization variable jointly. Note that the synchronization variable should be initialized by only one of the cooperating processes, as reinitializing a synchronization variable sets it to the *unlocked* state.

- Synchronization is the only way to ensure consistency of shared data.

- A process can map a file and have a thread in this process get a record's lock. When the modification is done, the thread releases the lock and unmaps the file. Once the lock is acquired, any other thread in any process mapping the file that tries to acquire the lock is blocked until the lock is released.

- Synchronization can ensure the safety of mutable data.

- Synchronization can be important even when accessing a single primitive variable, such as an integer. On machines where the integer is not aligned to the bus data width or is larger than the data width, a single memory load can use more than one memory cycle. While this cannot happen on the SPARC® architecture, portable programs cannot rely on this.

Mutual Exclusion Locks

Use mutual exclusion locks (mutexes) to serialize thread execution. Mutual exclusion locks synchronize threads, usually by ensuring that only one thread at a time executes a critical section of code. Mutex locks can also preserve single-threaded code.

Table 3-1   Routines for Mutual Exclusion Locks

Routine	Operation	Page
mutex_init(3T)	*Initialize a Mutual Exclusion Lock*	*page 37*
mutex_lock(3T)	*Lock a Mutex*	*page 37*
mutex_trylock(3T)	*Lock with a Nonblocking Mutex*	*page 38*
mutex_unlock(3T)	*Unlock a Mutex*	*page 38*
mutex_destroy(3T)	*Destroy Mutex State*	*page 39*

Mutexes can be used to synchronize threads in this process and other processes when they are allocated in memory that is writable and shared among the cooperating processes (see mmap(2)) and if they have been initialized for this behavior.

Mutexes must be initialized before use.

Note that there is no defined order of acquisition when multiple threads are waiting for a mutex.

Initialize a Mutual Exclusion Lock

mutex_init(3T)

```
#include <synch.h>   (or #include <thread.h>)

int mutex_init(mutex_t *mp, int type, void * arg);
```

Use mutex_init() to initialize the mutex pointed to by *mp*. The *type* can be one of the following (note that *arg* is currently ignored).

USYNC_PROCESS – The mutex can be used to synchronize threads in this and other processes.

USYNC_THREAD – The mutex can be used to synchronize threads in this process, only.

Mutexes can also be initialized by allocation in zeroed memory, in which case a *type* of USYNC_THREAD is assumed.

Multiple threads must not initialize the same mutex simultaneously. A mutex lock must not be reinitialized while other threads might be using it.

Return Values — mutex_init() returns zero after completing successfully. Any other returned value indicates that an error occurred. When any of the following conditions occur, the function fails and returns the corresponding value:

EINVAL   Invalid argument.

EFAULT   *mp* or *arg* points to an illegal address.

Lock a Mutex

mutex_lock(3T)

```
#include <synch.h>   (or #include <thread.h>)

int mutex_lock(mutex_t *mp);
```

Use mutex_lock() to lock the mutex pointed to by *mp*. When the mutex is already locked, the calling thread blocks until the mutex becomes available (blocked threads wait on a prioritized queue). When mutex_lock() returns, the mutex is locked and the calling thread is the owner.

Return Values — mutex_lock() returns zero after completing successfully. Any other returned value indicates that an error occurred. When any of the following conditions occur, the function fails and returns the corresponding value:

EINVAL   Invalid argument.

EFAULT   *mp* points to an illegal address.

Lock with a Nonblocking Mutex

mutex_trylock(3T)

```
#include <synch.h>   (or #include <thread.h>)

int mutex_trylock(mutex_t *mp);
```

Use mutex_trylock() to attempt to lock the mutex pointed to by *mp*. This function is a nonblocking version of mutex_lock(). When the mutex is already locked, this call returns with an error. Otherwise, the mutex is locked and the calling thread is the owner.

Return Values — mutex_trylock() returns zero after completing successfully. Any other returned value indicates that an error occurred. When any of the following conditions occur, the function fails and returns the corresponding value:

EINVAL   Invalid argument.

EFAULT   *mp* points to an illegal address.

EBUSY   The mutex pointed to by *mp* was already locked.

Unlock a Mutex

mutex_unlock(3T)

```
#include <synch.h>   (or #include <thread.h>)

int mutex_unlock(mutex_t *mp);
```

Use mutex_unlock() to unlock the mutex pointed to by *mp*. The mutex must be locked and the calling thread must be the one that last locked the mutex (the owner). When any other threads are waiting for the mutex to become available, the thread at the head of the queue is unblocked.

Return Values — mutex_unlock() returns zero after completing successfully. Any other returned value indicates that an error occurred. When any of the following conditions occur, the function fails and returns the corresponding value:

EINVAL   Invalid argument.

EFAULT   *mp* points to an illegal address.

Destroy Mutex State

mutex_destroy(3T)

```
#include <synch.h>  (or #include <thread.h>)

int mutex_destroy(mutex_t *mp);
```

Use mutex_destroy() to destroy any state associated with the mutex pointed to by *mp*. Note that the space for storing the mutex is not freed.

Return Values — mutex_destroy() returns zero after completing successfully. Any other returned value indicates that an error occurred. When any of the following conditions occur, the function fails and returns the corresponding value:

EINVAL   Invalid argument.

EFAULT   *mp* points to an illegal address.

Mutex Lock Code Example

Code Example 3-1   Mutex Lock Example

```
mutex_t count_mutex;
int count;

increment_count()
{
    mutex_lock(&count_mutex);
    count = count + 1;
    mutex_unlock(&count_mutex);
}

int
get_count()
{
    int c;

    mutex_lock(&count_mutex);
    c = count;
    mutex_unlock(&count_mutex);
    return (c);
}
```

The two functions in Code Example 3-1use the mutex lock for different purposes. increment_count() uses the mutex lock simply to assure an atomic[1] update of the shared variable. get_count() uses the mutex lock to guarantee that memory is synchronized when it refers to count.

---

1. An *atomic* operation cannot be divided into smaller operations.

Using Locking Hierarchies

You will occasionally want to access two resources at once. Perhaps you are using one of the resources, and then discover that the other resource is needed as well. As shown in Code Example 3-2, there could be a problem if two threads attempt to claim both resources but lock the associated mutexes in different orders. In this example, if the two threads lock mutexes 1 and 2 respectively, then a deadlock occurs when each attempts to lock the other mutex.

Code Example 3-2   Deadlock

Thread 1	Thread 2
`mutex_lock(&m1);`	`mutex_lock(&m2);`
`/* use resource 1 */`	`/* use resource 2 */`
`mutex_lock(&m2);`	`mutex_lock(&m1);`
`/* use resources` `1 and 2 */`	`/* use resources` `1 and 2 */`
`mutex_unlock(&m2);` `mutex_unlock(&m1);`	`mutex_unlock(&m1);` `mutex_unlock(&m2);`

The best way to avoid this problem is to make sure that whenever threads lock multiple mutexes, they do so in the same order. This technique is known as *lock hierarchies*: order the mutexes by logically assigning numbers to them.

Also, honor the restriction that you cannot take a mutex that is assigned i when you are holding any mutex assigned a number greater than i.

Note – The `lock_lint` tool can detect the sort of deadlock problem shown in this example. The best way to avoid such deadlock problems is to use lock hierarchies: when locks are always taken in a prescribed order, deadlock cannot occur.

However, this technique cannot always be used—sometimes you must take the mutexes in an order other than the prescribed one. To prevent deadlock in such a situation, one thread must release the mutexes it currently holds if it discovers that deadlock would otherwise be inevitable. Code Example 3-3 shows how this is done.

Code Example 3-3   Conditional Locking

Thread 1	Thread 2
| ```
mutex_lock(&m1);
    mutex_lock(&m2);

    mutex_unlock(&m2);

  mutex_unlock(&m1);
``` | ```
for (;;) {
    mutex_lock(&m2);
    if (mutex_trylock(&m1)
        ==0)
        /* got it! */
        break;

    /* didn't get it */
    mutex_unlock(&m2);
}
mutex_unlock(&m1);
mutex_unlock(&m2);
``` |

In this example, thread 1 is locking the mutexes in the prescribed order, but thread 2 is taking them out of order. To make certain that there is no deadlock, thread 2 has to take mutex 1 very carefully: if it were to block waiting for the mutex to be released, it is likely to have just entered into a deadlock with thread 1.

To make sure this does not happen, thread 2 calls `mutex_trylock`, which takes the mutex if it is available. If it is not, thread 2 returns immediately, reporting failure. At this point, thread 2 must release mutex 2, so that thread 1 can lock it, then release both mutex 1 and mutex 2.

Nested Locking With a Singly Linked List

Code Example 3-4 takes three locks at once, but prevents deadlock by taking the locks in a prescribed order.

Code Example 3-4   Singly Linked List Structure

```
typedef struct node1 {
   int value;
   struct node1 *link;
   mutex_t lock;
} node1_t;

node1_t ListHead;
```

This example uses a singly linked list structure with each node containing a mutex. To remove a node from the list, first search the list starting at ListHead (which itself is never removed) until the desired node is found.

To protect this search from the effects of concurrent deletions, lock each node before any of its contents can be accessed. Because all searches start at ListHead, there is never a deadlock because the locks are always taken in list order.

When the desired node is found, lock both the node and its predecessor because the change involves both nodes. Because the predecessor's lock is always taken first, you are again protected from deadlock.

Code Example 3-5 shows the C code to remove an item from a singly linked list.

Code Example 3-5   Singly Linked List with Nested Locking

```c
node1_t *delete(int value) {
    node1_t *prev, *curent;

    prev = &ListHead;
    mutex_lock(&prev->lock);
    while ((current = prev->link) != NULL) {
        mutex_lock(&current->lock);
        if (current->value == value) {
            prev->link = current->link;
            mutex_unlock(&current->lock);
            mutex_unlock(&prev->lock);
            current->link = NULL;
            return(current);
        }
        mutex_unlock(&prev->lock);
        prev = current;
    }
    mutex_unlock(&prev->lock);
    return(NULL);
}
```

Nested Locking With a Circular Linked List

Code Example 3-6 modifies the previous list structure by converting it into a circular list. There is no longer a distinguished head node; now a thread might be associated with a particular node and might perform operations on that node and its neighbor. Note that lock hierarchies do not work easily here because the obvious hierarchy (following the links) is circular.

Code Example 3-6   Circular Linked List Structure

```
typedef struct node2 {
    int value;
    struct node2 *link;
    mutex_t lock;
} node2_t;
```

Code Example 3-7 shows the C code that acquires the locks on two nodes and performs an operation involving both of them.

Code Example 3-7   Circular Linked List With Nested Locking

```
void Hit Neighbor(node2_t *me) {
    while (1) {
        mutex_lock(&me->lock);

        if (mutex_lock(&me->link->lock)) {
            /* failed to get lock */
            mutex_unlock(&me->lock);
            continue;
        }

        break;
    }
    me->link->value += me->value;
    me->value /=2;

    mutex_unlock(&me->link->lock);
    mutex_unlock(&me->lock);
}
```

Condition Variables

Use condition variables to atomically block threads until a particular condition is true. Always use condition variables together with a mutex lock.

Table 3-2   Routines for Condition Variables

Routine	Operation	Page
cond_init(3T)	*Initialize a Condition Variable*	*page 46*
cond_wait(3T)	*Block on a Condition Variable*	*page 46*
cond_signal(3T)	*Unblock a Specific Thread*	*page 48*
cond_timedwait(3T)	*Block Until a Specified Event*	*page 49*
cond_broadcast(3T)	*Unblock All Threads*	*page 51*
cond_destroy(3T)	*Destroy Condition Variable State*	*page 52*

With a condition variable, a thread can atomically block until a condition is satisfied. The condition is tested under the protection of a mutual exclusion lock (mutex).

When the condition is false, a thread usually blocks on a condition variable and atomically releases the mutex waiting for the condition to change. When another thread changes the condition, it can signal the associated condition variable to cause one or more waiting threads to wake up, reacquire the mutex, and re-evaluate the condition.

Condition variables can be used to synchronize threads among processes when they are allocated in memory that is writable and shared by the cooperating processes.

Always initialize condition variables before using them. Also, note that there is no defined order of unblocking when multiple threads are waiting for a condition variable.

Initialize a Condition Variable

cond_init(3T)

```
#include <synch.h>   (or #include <thread.h>)

int cond_init(cond_t *cvp, int type, int arg);
```

Use cond_init() to initialize the condition variable pointed to by *cvp*. The *type* can be one of the following (note that *arg* is currently ignored).

USYNC_PROCESS – The condition variable can be used to synchronize threads in this and other processes. *arg* is ignored.

USYNC_THREAD – The condition variable can be used to synchronize threads in this process, only. *arg* is ignored.

Condition variables can also be initialized by allocation in zeroed memory, in which case a type of USYNC_THREAD is assumed.

Multiple threads must not initialize the same condition variable simultaneously. A condition variable must not be reinitialized while other threads might be using it.

Return Values — cond_init() returns zero after completing successfully. Any other returned value indicates that an error occurred. When any of the following conditions occur, the function fails and returns the corresponding value:

EINVAL   *type* is not a recognized type.

EFAULT   *cvp* or *arg* points to an illegal address.

Block on a Condition Variable

cond_wait(3T)

```
#include <synch.h>   (or #include <thread.h>)

int cond_wait(cond_t *cvp, mutex_t *mp);
```

Use cond_wait() to atomically release the mutex pointed to by *mp* and to cause the calling thread to block on the condition variable pointed to by *cvp*. The blocked thread can be awakened by cond_signal(), cond_broadcast(), or when interrupted by delivery of a signal or a fork().

Any change in the value of a condition associated with the condition variable cannot be inferred by the return of cond_wait() and any such condition must be re-evaluated.

cond_wait() always returns with the mutex locked and owned by the calling thread even when returning an error.

The function blocks until the condition is signaled. It atomically releases the associated mutex lock before blocking, and atomically reacquires it before returning.

In typical use, a condition expression is evaluated under the protection of a mutex lock. When the condition expression is false, the thread blocks on the condition variable. The condition variable is then signaled by another thread when it changes the condition value. This causes one or all of the threads waiting on the condition to unblock and to try to reacquire the mutex lock.

Because the condition can change before an awakened thread returns from cond_wait(), the condition that caused the wait must be retested before the mutex lock is acquired. The recommended test method is to write the condition check as a while loop that calls cond_wait().

```
    mutex_lock();
        while(condition_is_false)
            cond_wait();
    mutex_unlock();
```

No specific order of acquisition is guaranteed when more than one thread blocks on the condition variable.

Return Values — cond_wait() returns zero after completing successfully. Any other returned value indicates that an error occurred. When any of the following conditions occur, the function fails and returns the corresponding value:

EFAULT   *cvp* points to an illegal address.

EINTR   The wait was interrupted by a signal or a fork().

3

Unblock a Specific Thread

cond_signal(3T)

```
#include <synch.h>  (or #include <thread.h>)

int cond_signal(cond_t *cvp);
```

Use cond_signal() to unblock one thread that is blocked on the condition variable pointed to by *cvp*. Call cond_signal() under the protection of the same mutex used with the condition variable being signaled. Otherwise, the condition variable could be signaled between the test of the associated condition and blocking in cond_wait(), which can cause an infinite wait.

When no threads are blocked on the condition variable, then cond_signal() has no effect.

Return Values — cond_signal() returns zero after completing successfully. Any other returned value indicates that an error occurred. When the following condition occurs, the function fails and returns the corresponding value:

EFAULT – *cvp* points to an illegal address.

Code Example 3-8   Example Using cond_wait(3T) and cond_signal(3T)

```
mutex_t count_lock;
cond_t count_nonzero;
unsigned int count;


decrement_count()
{
    mutex_lock(&count_lock);
    while (count == 0)
        cond_wait(&count_nonzero, &count_lock);
    count = count - 1;
    mutex_unlock(&count_lock);
}
increment_count()
{
    mutex_lock(&count_lock);
    if (count == 0)
        cond_signal(&count_nonzero);
    count = count + 1;
    mutex_unlock(&count_lock);
}
```

Block Until a Specified Event

cond_timedwait(3T)

```
#include <synch.h>  (or #include <thread.h>)

int cond_timedwait(cond_t *cvp, mutex_t *mp,
    timestruc_t *abstime);
```

Use cond_timedwait() as you would use cond_wait(), except that cond_timedwait() does not block past the time of day specified by *abstime*.

cond_timedwait() always returns with the mutex locked and owned by the calling thread even when returning an error.

The cond_timedwait() function blocks until the condition is signaled or until the time of day specified by the last argument has passed. The time-out is specified as a time of day so the condition can be retested efficiently without recomputing the time-out value, as shown in Code Example 3-9.

Return Values — cond_timedwait() returns zero after completing successfully. Any other returned value indicates that an error occurred. When any of the following conditions occur, the function fails and returns the corresponding value:

EINVAL   The specified number of seconds in *abstime* is greater than the start time of the application plus 50,000,000, or the number of nanoseconds is greater than or equal to 1,000,000,000.

EFAULT   *cvp* or *abstime* points to an illegal address.

EINTR   The wait was interrupted by a signal or a fork().

ETIME   The time specified by *abstime* has passed.

Code Example 3-9   Timed Condition Wait

```
timestruc_t to;
mutex_t m;
cond_t c;
...
mutex_lock(&m);
to.tv_sec = time(NULL) + TIMEOUT;
to.tv_nsec = 0;
while (cond == FALSE) {
    err = cond_timedwait(&c, &m, &to);
    if (err == ETIME) {
        /* timeout, do something */
        break;
    }
}
mutex_unlock(&m);
```

Unblock All Threads

cond_broadcast(3T)

```
#include <synch.h>  (or #include <thread.h>)

int cond_broadcast(cond_t *cvp);
```

Use cond_broadcast() to unblock all threads that are blocked on the condition variable pointed to by *cvp*. When no threads are blocked on the condition variable then cond_broadcast() has no effect.

This function wakes all the threads blocked in cond_wait(). Since cond_broadcast() causes all threads blocked on the condition to contend again for the mutex lock, use it with care.

For example, use cond_broadcast() to allow threads to contend for variable resource amounts when resources are freed, as shown in Code Example 3-10.

Code Example 3-10   Condition Variable Broadcast

```
mutex_t rsrc_lock;
cond_t rsrc_add;
unsigned int resources;

get_resources(int amount)
{
    mutex_lock(&rsrc_lock);
    while (resources < amount) {
        cond_wait(&rsrc_add, &rsrc_lock);
    }
    resources -= amount;
    mutex_unlock(&rsrc_lock);
}

add_resources(int amount)
{
    mutex_lock(&rsrc_lock);
    resources += amount;
    cond_broadcast(&rsrc_add);
    mutex_unlock(&rsrc_lock);
}
```

Note that in add_resources() it does not matter whether resources is updated first or cond_broadcast() is called first inside the mutex lock.

Return Values — cond_broadcast() returns zero after completing successfully. Any other returned value indicates that an error occurred. When any of the following condition occurs, the function fails and returns the corresponding value:

EFAULT – *cvp* points to an illegal address.

Call cond_broadcast() under the protection of the same mutex used with the condition variable being signaled. Otherwise, the condition variable could be signaled between the test of the associated condition and blocking in cond_wait(), which can cause an infinite wait.

Destroy Condition Variable State

cond_destroy(3T)

```
#include <synch.h>  (or #include <thread.h>)

int cond_destroy(cond_t *cvp);
```

Use cond_destroy() to destroy any state associated with the condition variable pointed to by *cvp*. The space for storing the condition variable is not freed.

Return Values — cond_destroy() returns zero after completing successfully. Any other returned value indicates that an error occurred. When the following condition occurs, the function fails and returns the corresponding value:

EFAULT – *cvp* points to an illegal address.

The Lost Wake-Up Problem

Calling cond_signal() or cond_broadcast() when the thread does not hold the mutex lock associated with the condition can lead to *lost wake-up* bugs. A lost wake up occurs when a signal or broadcast has been sent but a thread is waiting on the condition variable even though the condition is true. This happens when the thread that calls cond_signal() does not hold the mutex locally.

If the thread calls cond_signal() when another thread is between the test of the condition and the call to cond_wait(), there are no waiting threads and the signal has no effect.

The Producer/Consumer Problem

This problem is one of the small collection of standard, well-known problems in concurrent programming: a finite-size buffer and two classes of threads, *producers* and *consumers*, put items into the buffer (producers) and take items out of the buffer (consumers).

A producer must wait until the buffer has space before it can put something in, and a consumer must wait until something is in the buffer before it can take something out.

A condition variable represents a queue of threads waiting for some condition to be signaled.

Code Example 3-11 has two such queues, one (less) for producers waiting for a slot in the buffer, and the other (more) for consumers waiting for a buffer slot containing information. The example also has a mutex, as the data structure describing the buffer must be accessed by only one thread at a time.

This is the code for the buffer data structure.

Code Example 3-11   The Producer/Consumer Problem and Condition Variables

```
typedef struct {
    char buf[BSIZE];
    int occupied;
    int nextin;
    int nextout;
    mutex_t mutex;
    cond_t more;
    cond_t less;
} buffer_t;

buffer_t buffer;
```

As Code Example 3-12 on page 54 shows, the producer thread takes the mutex protecting the buffer data structure and then makes certain that space is available for the item being produced. If not, it calls cond_wait(), which causes it to join the queue of threads waiting for the condition less, representing *there is room in the buffer*, to be signaled.

At the same time, as part of the call to cond_wait(), the thread releases its lock on the mutex. The waiting producer threads depend on consumer threads to signal when the condition is true (as shown in Code Example 3-12). When the condition is signaled, the first thread waiting on less is awakened. However, before the thread can return from cond_wait(), it must reacquire the lock on the mutex.

This ensures that it again has mutually exclusive access to the buffer data structure. The thread then must check that there really is room available in the buffer; if so, it puts its item into the next available slot.

At the same time, consumer threads might be waiting for items to appear in the buffer. These threads are waiting on the condition variable more. A producer thread, having just deposited something in the buffer, calls cond_signal() to wake up the next waiting consumer. (If there are no waiting consumers, this call has no effect.) Finally, the producer thread unlocks the mutex, allowing other threads to operate on the buffer data structure.

Code Example 3-12   The Producer/Consumer Problem – the Producer

```
void producer(buffer_t *b, char item) {
    mutex_lock(&b->mutex);

    while (b->occupied >= BSIZE)
        cond_wait(&b->less, &b->mutex);

    assert(b->occupied < BSIZE);

    b->buf[b->nextin++] = item;

    b->nextin %= BSIZE;
    b->occupied++;

    /* now: either b->occupied < BSIZE and b->nextin is the index
       of the next empty slot in the buffer, or
       b->occupied == BSIZE and b->nextin is the index of the
       next (occupied) slot that will be emptied by a consumer
       (such as b->nextin == b->nextout) */

    cond_signal(&b->more);

    mutex_unlock(&b->mutex);
}
```

Note the use of the assert() statement; unless the code is compiled with NDEBUG defined, assert() does nothing when its argument evaluates to true (that is, non-zero), but causes the program to abort if the argument evaluates to false (zero).

Such assertions are especially useful in multithreaded programs—they immediately point out runtime problems if they fail, and they have the additional effect of being useful comments.

The code comment a few lines later could better be expressed as an assertion, but it is too complicated to say as a Boolean-valued expression and so is said here in English.

Both the assertion and the comments are examples of *invariants*. These are logical statements that should not be falsified by the execution of the program, except during brief moments when a thread is modifying some of the program variables mentioned in the invariant. (An assertion, of course, should be true whenever any thread executes it.)

Using invariants is an extremely useful technique. Even when they are not stated in the program text, think in terms of invariants when you analyze a program.

The invariant in the producer code that is expressed as a comment is always true whenever a thread is in the part of the code where the comment appears. If you move this comment to just after the mutex_unlock(), this does not necessarily remain true. If you move this comment to just after the assert, this is still true.

The point is that this invariant expresses a property that is true at all times, except when either a producer or a consumer is changing the state of the buffer. While a thread is operating on the buffer (under the protection of a mutex), it might temporarily falsify the invariant. However, once the thread is finished, the invariant should be true again.

Code Example 3-13 shows the code for the consumer. Its flow is symmetric with that of the producer.

Code Example 3-13   The Producer/Consumer Problem – the Consumer

```
char consumer(buffer_t *b) {
    char item;
    mutex_lock(&b->mutex);
    while(b->occupied <= 0)
        cond_wait(&b->more, &b->mutex);

    assert(b->occupied > 0);

    item = b->buf[b->nextout++];
    b->nextout %= BSIZE;
    b->occupied--;

    /* now: either b->occupied > 0 and b->nextout is the index
       of the next occupied slot in the buffer, or
       b->occupied == 0 and b->nextout is the index of the next
       (empty) slot that will be filled by a producer (such as
       b->nextout == b->nextin) */

    cond_signal(&b->less);
    mutex_unlock(&b->mutex);

    return(item);
}
```

Multiple-Readers, Single-Writer Locks

Readers/Writer locks allow simultaneous read access by many threads while restricting write access to only one thread at a time.

Table 3-3   Routines for Readers/Writer Locks

Routine	Operation	Page
rwlock_init(3T)	*Initialize a Readers/Writer Lock*	*page 58*
rw_rdlock(3T)	*Acquire a Read Lock*	*page 58*
rw_tryrdlock(3T)	*Try to Acquire a Read Lock*	*page 59*
rw_wrlock(3T)	*Acquire a Write Lock*	*page 59*
rw_trywrlock(3T)	*Try to Acquire a Write Lock*	*page 60*
rw_unlock(3T)	*Unlock a Readers/Writer Lock*	*page 60*
rwlock_destroy(3T)	*Destroy Readers/Writer Lock State*	*page 61*

When any thread holds the lock for reading, other threads can also acquire the lock for reading but must wait to acquire the lock for writing. If one thread holds the lock for writing, or is waiting to acquire the lock for writing, other threads must wait to acquire the lock for either reading or writing.

Readers/Writer locks are slower than mutexes, but can improve performance when they protect data that are not frequently written but that are read by many concurrent threads.

Use readers/writer locks to synchronize threads in this process and other processes by allocating them in memory that is writable and shared among the cooperating processes (see mmap(2)) and by initializing them for this behavior.

By default, the acquisition order is not defined when multiple threads are waiting for a readers/writer lock. However, to avoid writer starvation, the Solaris threads package tends to favor writers over readers.

Readers/Writer locks must be initialized before use.

Initialize a Readers/Writer Lock

rwlock_init(3T)

```
#include <synch.h>   (or #include <thread.h>)

int rwlock_init(rwlock_t *rwlp, int type, void * arg);
```

Use `rwlock_init()` to initialize the readers/writer lock pointed to by `rwlp` and to set the lock state to unlocked. *type* can be one of the following (note that *arg* is currently ignored).

USYNC_PROCESS – The readers/writer lock can be used to synchronize threads in this process and other processes. *arg* is ignored.

USYNC_THREAD – The readers/writer lock can be used to synchronize threads in this process, only. *arg* is ignored.

Multiple threads must not initialize the same readers/writer lock simultaneously. Readers/Writer locks can also be initialized by allocation in zeroed memory, in which case a type of USYNC_THREAD is assumed. A readers/writer lock must not be reinitialized while other threads might be using it.

Return Values — rwlock_init() returns zero after completing successfully. Any other returned value indicates that an error occurred. When any of the following conditions occur, the function fails and returns the corresponding value:

EINVAL   Invalid argument

EFAULT   *rwlp* or *arg* points to an illegal address.

Acquire a Read Lock

rw_rdlock(3T)

```
#include <synch.h>   (or #include <thread.h>)

int rw_rdlock(rwlock_t *rwlp);
```

Use `rw_rdlock()` to acquire a read lock on the readers/writer lock pointed to by *rwlp*. When the readers/writer lock is already locked for writing, the calling thread blocks until the write lock is released. Otherwise, the read lock is acquired.

Return Values — rw_rdlock() returns zero after completing successfully. Any other returned value indicates that an error occurred. When any of the following conditions occur, the function fails and returns the corresponding value:

EINVAL   Invalid argument.

EFAULT   *rwlp* points to an illegal address.

Try to Acquire a Read Lock

rw_tryrdlock(3T)

```
#include <synch.h>   (or #include <thread.h>)

int rw_tryrdlock(rwlock_t *rwlp);
```

Use rw_tryrdlock() to attempt to acquire a read lock on the readers/writer lock pointed to by *rwlp*. When the readers/writer lock is already locked for writing, it returns an error. Otherwise, the read lock is acquired.

Return Values — rw_tryrdlock() returns zero after completing successfully. Any other returned value indicates that an error occurred. When any of the following conditions occur, the function fails and returns the corresponding value:

EINVAL   Invalid argument.

EFAULT   *rwlp* points to an illegal address.

EBUSY   The readers/writer lock pointed to by *rwlp* was already locked.

Acquire a Write Lock

rw_wrlock(3T)

```
#include <synch.h>   (or #include <thread.h>)

int rw_wrlock(rwlock_t *rwlp);
```

Use rw_wrlock() to acquire a write lock on the readers/writer lock pointed to by *rwlp*. When the readers/writer lock is already locked for reading or writing, the calling thread blocks until all the read locks and write locks are released. Only one thread at a time can hold a write lock on a readers/writer lock.

Return Values — rw_wrlock() returns zero after completing successfully. Any other returned value indicates that an error occurred. When any of the following conditions occur, the function fails and returns the corresponding value:

EINVAL   Invalid argument.

EFAULT   *rwlp* points to an illegal address.

Try to Acquire a Write Lock

rw_trywrlock(3T)

```
#include <synch.h>   (or #include <thread.h>)

int rw_trywrlock(rwlock_t *rwlp);
```

Use rw_trywrlock() to attempt to acquire a write lock on the readers/writer lock pointed to by *rwlp*. When the readers/writer lock is already locked for reading or writing, it returns an error.

Return Values — rw_trywrlock() returns zero after completing successfully. Any other returned value indicates that an error occurred. When any of the following conditions occur, the function fails and returns the corresponding value:

EINVAL Invalid argument.

EFAULT *rwlp* points to an illegal address.

EBUSY The readers/writer lock pointed to by *rwlp* was already locked.

Unlock a Readers/Writer Lock

rw_unlock(3T)

```
#include <synch.h>   (or #include <thread.h>)

int rw_unlock(rwlock_t *rwlp);
```

Use rw_unlock() to unlock a readers/writer lock pointed to by *rwlp*. The readers/writer lock must be locked and the calling thread must hold the lock either for reading or writing. When any other threads are waiting for the readers/writer lock to become available, one of them is unblocked.

Return Values — rw_unlock() returns zero after completing successfully. Any other returned value indicates that an error occurred. When any of the following conditions occur, the function fails and returns the corresponding value:

EINVAL   Invalid argument.

EFAULT   *rwlp* points to an illegal address.

Destroy Readers/Writer Lock State

rwlock_destroy(3T)

```
#include <synch.h>   (or #include <thread.h>)

int rwlock_destroy(rwlock_t *rwlp);
```

Use rwlock_destroy() to destroy any state associated with the readers/writer lock pointed to by *rlwp*. The space for storing the readers/writer lock is not freed.

Return Values — rwlock_destroy() returns zero after completing successfully. Any other returned value indicates that an error occurred. When any of the following conditions occur, the function fails and returns the corresponding value:

EINVAL   Invalid argument.

EFAULT   *rwlp* points to an illegal address.

Code Example 3-14 uses a bank account to demonstrate readers/writer locks. While the program could allow multiple threads to have concurrent read-only access to the account balance, only a single writer is allowed. Note that the get_balance() function needs the lock to ensure that the addition of the checking and saving balances occurs atomically.

Code Example 3-14   Read/Write Bank Account

```
rwlock_t account_lock;
float checking_balance = 100.0;
float saving_balance = 100.0;
...
rwlock_init(&account_lock, 0, NULL);
...
float
get_balance() {
    float bal;

    rw_rdlock(&account_lock);
    bal = checking_balance + saving_balance;
    rw_unlock(&account_lock);
    return(bal);
}

void
transfer_checking_to_savings(float amount) {
    rw_wrlock(&account_lock);
    checking_balance = checking_balance - amount;
    savings_balance = savings_balance + amount;
    rw_unlock(&account_lock);
}
```

Semaphores

Semaphores are a programming construct designed by E. W. Dijkstra in the late 1960s. Dijkstra's model was the operation of railroads: consider a stretch of railroad in which there is a single track over which only one train at a time is allowed.

Guarding this track is a semaphore. A train must wait before entering the single track until the semaphore is in a state that permits travel. When the train enters the track, the semaphore changes state to prevent other trains from entering the track. A train that is leaving this section of track must again change the state of the semaphore to allow another train to enter.

In the computer version, a semaphore appears to be a simple integer. A thread waits for permission to proceed and then signals that it has proceeded by performing a P operation on the semaphore.

The semantics of the operation are such that the thread must wait until the semaphore's value is positive, then change the semaphore's value by subtracting one from it. When it is finished, the thread performs a V operation, which changes the semaphore's value by adding one to it. It is crucial that these operations take place *atomically*—they cannot be subdivided into pieces between which other actions on the semaphore can take place. In the P operation, the semaphore's value must be positive just before it is decremented (resulting in a value that is guaranteed to be non-negative and one less than what it was before it was decremented).

In both P and V operations, the arithmetic must take place without interference. If two V operations are performed simultaneously on the same semaphore, the net effect should be that the semaphore's new value is two greater than it was.

The mnemonic significance of P and V is lost on most of the world, as Dijkstra is Dutch. However, in the interest of true scholarship: P stands for *prolagen*, a made-up word derived from *proberen te verlagen*, which means *try to decrease*. V stands for *verhogen*, which means *increase*. This is discussed in one of Dijkstra's technical notes, *EWD 74*.

sema_wait(3T) and sema_post(3T) correspond to Dijkstra's P and V operations. sema_trywait(3T) is a conditional form of the P operation: if the calling thread cannot decrement the value of the semaphore without waiting, the call returns immediately with a non-zero value.

There are two basic sorts of semaphores: *binary* semaphores, which never take on values other than zero or one, and *counting* semaphores, which can take on arbitrary non-negative values. A binary semaphore is logically just like a mutex.

However, although it is not enforced, mutexes should be unlocked only by the thread holding the lock. There is no notion of "the thread holding the semaphore," so any thread can perform a V (or sema_post(3T)) operation.

3

Counting semaphores are about as powerful as conditional variables (used in conjunction with mutexes). In many cases, the code might be simpler when it is implemented with counting semaphores rather than with condition variables (as shown in the next few examples).

However, when a mutex is used with condition variables, there is an implied bracketing—it is clear which part of the program is being protected. This is not necessarily the case for a semaphore, which might be called the *go to* of concurrent programming—it is powerful but too easy to use in an unstructured, unfathomable way.

Counting Semaphores

Conceptually, a semaphore is a non-negative integer count. Semaphores are typically used to coordinate access to resources, with the semaphore count initialized to the number of free resources. Threads then atomically increment the count when resources are added and atomically decrement the count when resources are removed.

When the semaphore count becomes zero, indicating that no more resources are present, threads trying to decrement the semaphore block until the count becomes greater than zero.

Table 3-4   Routines for Semaphores

Routine	Operation	Page
sema_init(3T)	*Initialize a Semaphore*	*page 65*
sema_post(3T)	*Increment a Semaphore*	*page 65*
sema_wait(3T)	*Block on a Semaphore Count*	*page 66*
sema_trywait(3T)	*Decrement a Semaphore Count*	*page 66*
sema_destroy(3T)	*Destroy the Semaphore State*	*page 67*

Because semaphores need not be acquired and released by the same thread, they can be used for asynchronous event notification (such as in signal handlers). And, because semaphores contain state, they can be used asynchronously without acquiring a mutex lock as is required by condition variables. However, semaphores are not as efficient as mutex locks.

By default, there is no defined order of unblocking if multiple threads are waiting for a semaphore.

Semaphores must be initialized before use.

Initialize a Semaphore

sema_init(3T)

```
#include <synch.h>    (or #include <thread.h>)

int sema_init(sema_t *sp, unsigned int count,int type, void * arg);
```

Use sema_init() to initialize the semaphore variable pointed to by *sp* by *count* amount. *type* can be one of the following (note that *arg* is currently ignored).

USYNC_PROCESS – The semaphore can be used to synchronize threads in this process and other processes. Only one process should initialize the semaphore. *arg* is ignored.

USYNC_THREAD – The semaphore can be used to synchronize threads in this process, only. *arg* is ignored.

Multiple threads must not initialize the same semaphore simultaneously. A semaphore must not be reinitialized while other threads may be using it.

Return Values — sema_init() returns zero after completing successfully. Any other returned value indicates that an error occurred. When any of the following conditions occur, the function fails and returns the corresponding value:

EINVAL   Invalid argument.

EFAULT   *sp* or *arg* points to an illegal address.

Increment a Semaphore

sema_post(3T)

```
#include <synch.h>    (or #include <thread.h>)

int sema_post(sema_t *sp)
```

Use sema_post() to atomically increment the semaphore pointed to by *sp*. When any threads are blocked on the semaphore, one is unblocked.

Return Values — sema_post() returns zero after completing successfully. Any other returned value indicates that an error occurred. When any of the following conditions occur, the function fails and returns the corresponding value:

EINVAL   Invalid argument.

EFAULT   *sp* points to an illegal address.

Block on a Semaphore Count

sema_wait(3T)

```
#include <synch.h>    (or #include <thread.h>)

int sema_wait(sema_t *sp)
```

Use sema_wait() to block the calling thread until the count in the semaphore pointed to by *sp* becomes greater than zero, then atomically decrement it.

Return Values — sema_wait() returns zero after completing successfully. Any other returned value indicates that an error occurred. When any of the following conditions occur, the function fails and returns the corresponding value:

EINVAL   Invalid argument.

EFAULT   *sp* points to an illegal address.

EINTR   The wait was interrupted by a signal or a fork().

Decrement a Semaphore Count

sema_trywait(3T)

```
#include <synch.h>    (or #include <thread.h>)

int sema_trywait(sema_t *sp)
```

Use sema_trywait() to atomically decrement the count in the semaphore pointed to by *sp* when the count is greater than zero. This function is a nonblocking version of sema_wait().

Return Values — sema_trywait() returns zero after completing successfully. Any other returned value indicates that an error occurred. When any of the following conditions occur, the function fails and returns the corresponding value:

EINVAL   Invalid argument.

EFAULT   *sp* points to an illegal address.

EBUSY   The semaphore pointed to by *sp* has a zero count.

Destroy the Semaphore State

sema_destroy(3T)

```
#include <synch.h>    (or #include <thread.h>)

int sema_destroy(sema_t *sp)
```

Use sema_destroy() to destroy any state associated with the semaphore pointed to by *sp*. The space for storing the semaphore is not freed.

Return Values — sema_destroy() returns zero after completing successfully. Any other returned value indicates that an error occurred. When any of the following conditions occur, the function fails and returns the corresponding value:

EINVAL   Invalid argument.

EFAULT   *sp* points to an illegal address.

The Producer/Consumer Problem, Using Semaphores

The data structure in Code Example 3-15 is similar to that used for the solution with condition variables; two semaphores represent the number of full and empty buffers and ensure that producers wait until there are empty buffers and that consumers wait until there are full buffers.

Code Example 3-15   The Producer/Consumer Problem with Semaphores

```
typedef struct {
    char buf[BSIZE];
    sema_t occupied;
    sema_t empty;
    int nextin;
    int nextout;
    sema_t pmut;
    sema_t cmut;
} buffer_t;

buffer_t buffer;

sema_init(&buffer.occupied, 0, USYNC_THREAD, 0);
sema_init(&buffer.empty, BSIZE, USYNC_THREAD, 0);
sema_init(&buffer.pmut, 1, USYNC_THREAD, 0);
sema_init(&buffer.cmut, 1, USYNC_THREAD, 0);
buffer.nextin = buffer.nextout = 0;
```

Another pair of (binary) semaphores plays the same role as mutexes, controlling access to the buffer when there are multiple producers and multiple empty buffer slots, and when there are multiple consumers and multiple full buffer slots. Mutexes would work better here, but would not provide as good an example of semaphore use.

Code Example 3-16   The Producer/Consumer Problem – the Producer

```
void producer(buffer_t *b, char item) {
    sema_wait(&b->empty);

    sema_wait(&b->pmut);

    b->buf[b->nextin] = item;
    b->nextin++;
    b->nextin %= BSIZE;

    sema_post(&b->pmut);

    sema_post(&b->occupied);
}
```

Code Example 3-17   The Producer/Consumer Problem – the Consumer

```
char consumer(buffer_t *b) {
    char item;

    sema_wait(&b->occupied);

    sema_wait(&b->cmut);

    item = b->buf[b->nextout];
    b->nextout++;
    b->nextout %= BSIZE;

    sema_post(&b->cmut);

    sema_post(&b->empty);

    return(item);
}
```

3

Synchronization Across Process Boundaries

Each of the four synchronization primitives can be set up to be used across process boundaries. This is done quite simply by ensuring that the synchronization variable is located in a shared memory segment and by calling the appropriate init routine with *type* set to USYNC_PROCESS. If this has been done, then the operations on the synchronization variables work just as they do when *type* is USYNC_THREAD.

```
mutex_init(&m, USYNC_PROCESS, 0);

rwlock_init(&rw, USYNC_PROCESS, 0);

cond_init(&cv, USYNC_PROCESS, 0);

sema_init(&s, count, USYNC_PROCESS, 0);
```

Code Example 3-18 shows the producer/consumer problem with the producer and consumer in separate processes. The main routine maps zero-filled memory (that it shares with its child process) into its address space. Note that mutex_init() and cond_init() must be called because the type of the synchronization variables is USYNC_PROCESS.

A child process is created that runs the consumer. The parent runs the producer.

This example also shows the drivers for the producer and consumer. The producer_driver() simply reads characters from stdin and calls producer(). The consumer_driver() gets characters by calling consumer() and writes them to stdout.

Code Example 3-18 The Producer/Consumer Problem, Using USYNC_PROCESS

```
main() {
    int zfd;
    buffer_t *buffer;

    zfd = open("/dev/zero", O_RDWR);
    buffer = (buffer_t *)mmap(NULL, sizeof(buffer_t),
        PROT_READ|PROT_WRITE, MAP_SHARED, zfd, 0);
    buffer->occupied = buffer->nextin = buffer->nextout = 0;

    mutex_init(&buffer->lock, USYNC_PROCESS, 0);
    cond_init(&buffer->less, USYNC_PROCESS, 0);
    cond_init(&buffer->more, USYNC_PROCESS, 0);
    if (fork() == 0)
        consumer_driver(buffer);
    else
        producer_driver(buffer);
}

void producer_driver(buffer_t *b) {
    int item;

    while (1) {
        item = getchar();
        if (item == EOF) {
            producer(b, '\0');
            break;
        } else
            producer(b, (char)item);
    }
}

void consumer_driver(buffer_t *b) {
    char item;

    while (1) {
        if ((item = consumer(b)) == '\0')
            break;
        putchar(item);
    }
}
```

3

A child process is created to run the consumer; the parent runs the producer.

Comparing Primitives

The most basic synchronization primitive in Solaris threads is the mutual exclusion lock. So, it is the most efficient mechanism in both memory use and execution time. The basic use of a mutual exclusion lock is to serialize access to a resource.

The next most efficient primitive in Solaris threads is the condition variable. The basic use of a condition variable is to block on a change of state. Remember that a mutex lock must be acquired before blocking on a condition variable and must be unlocked after returning from cond_wait() and after changing the state of the variable.

The semaphore uses more memory than the condition variable. It is easier to use in some circumstances because a semaphore variable functions on state rather than on control. Unlike a lock, a semaphore does not have an owner. Any thread can increment a semaphore that has blocked.

The readers/writer lock is the most complex Solaris threads synchronization mechanism. This means that the readers/writer lock is most efficiently used with a much coarser granularity than is effective with the other synchronization primitives. A readers/writer lock is basically used with a resource whose contents are searched more often than they are changed.

Programming with the Operating System

System 4 ≡

This chapter describes how multithreading interacts with the Solaris operating system and how the operating system has changed to support multithreading.

Processes – Changes for Multithreading

Duplicating Parent Threads

fork(2)

With the fork(2) and fork1(2) functions, you can choose between duplicating all parent threads in the child or only one parent thread in the child.

The fork() function duplicates the address space and all the threads (and LWPs) in the child. This is useful, for example, when the child process never calls exec(2) but does use its copy of the parent address space.

To illustrate, think about a thread in the parent process—other than the one that called fork()—that has locked a mutex. This mutex is copied into the child process in its locked state, but no thread is copied over to unlock the mutex. So, any thread in the child that tries to lock the mutex waits forever. To avoid this sort of situation, use fork() to duplicate all the threads in the process.

Note that when one thread in a process calls fork(), threads blocked in an interruptible system call will return EINTR.

fork1(2)

The fork1(2)[1] function duplicates the complete address space in the child but duplicates only the thread that called fork1(). This is useful when the child process immediately calls exec(), which is what happens after most calls to fork(). In this case, the child process does not need a duplicate of any thread other than the one that called fork(2).

Do not call any library functions after calling fork1() and before calling exec()—one of the library functions might use a lock that is held by more than one thread.

Cautions for Both fork(2) and fork1(2)

For both fork() and fork1(), be careful when you use global state after a call to either.

For example, when one thread reads a file serially and another thread in the process successfully calls fork(), each process then contains a thread that is reading the file. Because the seek pointer for a file descriptor is shared after a fork(), the thread in the parent gets some data while the thread in the child gets the rest.

Also for both fork() and fork1(), be careful not to create locks that are held by both the parent and child processes. This can happen when locks are allocated in memory that is sharable (that is mmap(2)'ed with the MAP_SHARED flag).

vfork(2)

vfork(2) is like fork1() in that only the calling thread is copied in the child process. As in nonthreaded implementations, vfork() does not copy the address space for the child process.

Be careful that the thread in the child process does not change memory before it calls exec(2). Remember that vfork() gives the parent address space to the child. The parent gets its address space back after the child calls exec() or exits. It is important that the child not change the state of the parent.

For example, it is dangerous to create new threads between the call to vfork() and the call to exec().

---

1. Terminology will probably change when POSIX 1003.4a is adopted. What is currently called fork(2) will be called forkall(), and what is called fork1(2) will be called fork(). Also added in POSIX is the idea of the "fork cleanup handler"— you can call pthread_atfork() to register three functions to be called, respectively, just before the fork() takes place, and just after the fork() in both the parent and the child processes. These routines are to clean up locks and so on, although this is necessary only with the version of fork() that creates only one thread in the child process.

Executing Files and Terminating Processes

exec(2) and exit(2)

Both the exec(2) and exit(2) system calls work as they do in single-thread processes except that they destroy all the threads in the address space. Both calls block until all the execution resources (and so all active threads) are destroyed.

When exec() rebuilds the process, it creates a single LWP. The process start-up code builds the initial thread. As usual, if the initial thread returns it calls exit() and the process is destroyed.

When all the threads in a process exit, the process itself exits with a status of zero.

Alarms, Interval Timers, and Profiling

Each LWP has a unique realtime interval timer and alarm that a thread bound to the LWP can use. The timer or alarm delivers one signal to the thread when the timer or alarm expires.

Each LWP also has a virtual time or profile interval timer that a thread bound to the LWP can use. When the interval timer expires, either SIGVTALRM or SIGPROF, as appropriate, is sent to the LWP that owns the interval timer.

You can profile each LWP with profil(2), giving each LWP its own buffer or sharing buffers between LWPs. Profiling data is updated at each clock tick in LWP user time. The profile state is inherited from the creating LWP.

Non-local Goto – setjmp(3C) and longjmp(3C)

The scope of setjmp() and longjmp() is limited to one thread, which is fine most of the time. However, this does mean that a thread that handles a signal can longjmp() only when setjmp() is performed in the same thread.

Resource Limits

Resource limits are set on the entire process and are determined by adding the resource use of all threads in the process. When a soft resource limit is exceeded, the offending thread is sent the appropriate signal. The sum of the resource use in the process is available through getrusage(3B).

LWPs and Scheduling Classes

The Solaris kernel has three classes of process scheduling. The highest priority scheduling class is realtime (RT). The middle priority scheduling class is system. The system scheduling class cannot be applied to a user process. The lowest priority scheduling class is timeshare (TS), which is also the default class.

Scheduling class is maintained for each LWP. When a process is created, the initial LWP inherits the scheduling class and priority of the parent process. As more LWPs are created to run unbound threads, they also inherit this scheduling class and priority. All unbound threads in a process have the same scheduling class and priority.

Each scheduling class maps the priority of the LWP it is scheduling to an overall dispatching priority according to the configurable priority of the scheduling class.

Bound threads have the scheduling class and priority of their underlying LWPs. Each bound thread in a process can have a unique scheduling class and priority that is visible to the kernel. Bound threads are scheduled with respect to all other LWPs in the system.

The scheduling class is set by priocntl(2). How you specify the first two arguments determines whether just the calling LWP or all the LWPs of one or more processes are affected. The third argument of priocntl() is the command, which can be one of the following.

- PC_GETCID – Get the class ID and class attributes for a specific class.

- PC_GETCLINFO – Get the class name and class attributes for a specific class.

- PC_GETPARMS – Get the class identifier and the class-specific scheduling parameters of a process, an LWP with a process, or a group of processes.

- PC_SETPARMS – Set the class identifier and the class-specific scheduling parameters of a process, an LWP with a process, or a group of processes.

Use priocntl() only on bound threads. To affect the priority of unbound threads, use thr_setprio(3T).

Timeshare Scheduling

Timeshare scheduling fairly distributes the processing resource to the set of processes. Other parts of the kernel can monopolize the processor for short intervals without degrading response time as seen by the user.

The priocntl(2) call sets the nice(2) level of one or more processes. priocntl() affects the nice() level of all the timesharing class LWPs in the process. The nice() level ranges from 0 to +20 normally and from -20 to +20 for processes with superuser privilege. The lower the value, the higher the priority.

The dispatch priority of time-shared LWPs is calculated from the instantaneous CPU use rate of the LWP and from its nice() level. The nice() level indicates the relative priority of the processes to the timeshare scheduler. LWPs with a greater nice() value get a smaller, but non-zero, share of the total processing. An LWP that has received a larger amount of processing is given lower priority than one that has received little or no processing.

Realtime Scheduling

The realtime class (RT) can be applied to a whole process or to one or more LWPs in a process. This requires superuser privilege. Unlike the nice(2) level of the timeshare class, LWPs that are classified realtime can be assigned priorities either individually or jointly. A priocntl(2) call affects the attributes of all the realtime LWPs in the process.

The scheduler always dispatches the highest-priority realtime LWP. It preempts a lower-priority LWP when a higher-priority LWP becomes runnable. A preempted LWP is placed at the head of its level queue. A realtime LWP retains control of a processor until it is preempted, it suspends, or its realtime priority is changed. LWPs in the RT class have absolute priority over processes in the TS class.

A new LWP inherits the scheduling class of the parent process or LWP. An RT class LWP inherits the parent's time slice, whether finite or infinite. An LWP with a finite time slice runs until it terminates, blocks (for example, to wait for an I/O event), is preempted by a higher-priority runnable realtime process, or the time slice expires. An LWP with an infinite time slice ceases execution only when it terminates, blocks, or is preempted.

LWP Scheduling and Thread Binding

The threads library automatically adjusts the number of LWPs in the pool used to run unbound threads. Its objectives are:

- To prevent the program from being blocked by a lack of unblocked LWPs
  For example, if there are more runnable unbound threads than LWPs and all the active threads block in the kernel in indefinite waits (such as reading a tty), the process cannot progress until a waiting thread returns.

- To make efficient use of LWPs
  For example, if the library creates one LWP for each thread, many LWPs will usually be idle and the operating system is overloaded by the resource requirements of the unused LWPs.

Keep in mind that LWPs are time-sliced, not threads. This means that when there is only one LWP there is no time slicing within the process—threads run on the LWP until they block (through inter-thread synchronization), are preempted, or terminate.

You can assign priorities to threads with `thr_setprio`(3T): lower-priority unbound threads are assigned to LWPs only when no higher-priority unbound threads are available. Bound threads, of course, do not compete for LWPs because they have their own.

Bind threads to your LWPs to get precise control over whatever is being scheduled. This control is not possible when many unbound threads compete for an LWP.

Realtime threads are useful for getting a quick response to external stimuli. Consider a thread used for mouse tracking that must respond instantly to mouse clicks. By binding the thread to an LWP, you guarantee that there is an LWP available when it is needed. By assigning the LWP to the realtime scheduling class, you ensure that the LWP is scheduled quickly in response to mouse clicks.

SIGWAITING—Creating LWPs for Waiting Threads

The library usually ensures that there are enough LWPs in its pool for a program to proceed. When all the LWPs in the process are blocked in indefinite waits (such as blocked reading from a tty or network), the operating system sends the new signal, SIGWAITING, to the process. This signal is handled by the threads library. When the process contains a thread that is waiting to run, a new LWP is created and the appropriate waiting thread is assigned to it for execution.

The SIGWAITING mechanism does not ensure that an additional LWP is created when one or more threads are compute bound and another thread becomes runnable. A compute-bound thread can prevent multiple runnable threads from being started because of a shortage of LWPs. This can be prevented by calling `thr_setconcurrency`(3T) or by using THR_NEW_LWP in calls to `thr_create`(3T).

Aging LWPs

When the number of active threads is reduced, some of the LWPs in the pool are no longer needed. When there are more LWPs than active threads, the threads library destroys the unneeded ones. The library ages LWPs—they are deleted when they are unused for a "long" time, currently set at five minutes.

Extending Traditional Signals

The traditional UNIX signal model is extended to threads in a fairly natural way. The disposition of signals is established process-wide, using the traditional mechanisms (signal(2), sigaction(2), and so on).

When a signal handler is marked SIG_DFL or SIG_IGN, the action on receipt of the signal (exit, core dump, stop, continue, or ignore) is performed on the entire receiving process, affecting all threads in the process. See signal(5) for basic information about signals.

Each thread has its own signal mask. This lets a thread block some signals while it uses memory or other state that is also used by a signal handler. All threads in a process share the set of signal handlers set up by sigaction(2) and its variants, as usual.

A thread in one process cannot send a signal to a specific thread in another process. A signal sent by kill(2) or sigsend(2) is to a process and is handled by any one of the receptive threads in the process.

Unbound threads cannot use alternate signal stacks. A bound thread can use an alternate stack because the state is associated with the execution resource. An alternate stack must be enabled for the signal through sigaction(2), and declared and enabled through sigaltstack(2).

An application can have per-thread signal handlers based on the per-process signal handlers. One way is for the process-wide signal handler to use the identifier of the thread handling the signal as an index into a table of per-thread handlers. Note that there is no thread zero.

Signals are divided into two categories: traps and exceptions (synchronous signals) and interrupts (asynchronous signals).

As in traditional UNIX, if a signal is pending, additional occurrences of that signal have no additional effect—a pending signal is represented by a bit, not a counter.

As is the case with single-threaded processes, when a thread receives a signal while blocked in a system call, the thread might return early, either with the EINTR error code, or, in the case of I/O calls, with fewer bytes transferred than requested.

Of particular importance to multithreaded programs is the effect of signals on cond_wait(3T). This call usually returns in response to a cond_signal(3T) or a cond_broadcast(3T), but, if the waiting thread receives a UNIX signal, it returns with the error code EINTR. See "Interrupted Waits on Condition Variables" on page 86 for more information.

Synchronous Signals

Traps (such as SIGILL, SIGFPE, SIGSEGV) result from something a thread does to itself, such as dividing by zero or explicitly sending itself a signal. A trap is handled only by the thread that caused it. Several threads in a process can generate and handle the same type of trap simultaneously.

Extending the idea of signals to individual threads is easy for synchronous signals—the signal is dealt with by the thread that caused the problem. However, if the thread has not chosen to deal with the problem, such as by establishing a signal handler with sigaction(2), the entire process is terminated.

Because such a synchronous signal usually means that something is seriously wrong with the whole process, and not just with a thread, terminating the process is often a good choice.

Asynchronous Signals

Interrupts (such as SIGINT and SIGIO) are asynchronous with any thread and result from some action outside the process. They might be signals sent explicitly by other threads, or they might represent external actions such as a user typing Control-C. Dealing with asynchronous signals is more complicated than dealing with synchronous signals.

An interrupt can be handled by any thread whose signal mask allows it. When more than one thread is able to receive the interrupt, only one is chosen.

When multiple occurrences of the same signal are sent to a process, then each occurrence can be handled by a separate thread, as long as threads are available that do not have it masked. When all threads have the signal masked, then the signal is marked *pending* and the first thread to unmask the signal handles it.

Continuation Semantics

Continuation semantics are the traditional way to deal with signals. The idea is that when a signal handler returns, control resumes where it was at the time of the interruption. This is well suited for asynchronous signals in single-threaded processes, as shown in Code Example 4-1. This is also used as the exception-handling mechanism in some programming languages, such as PL/1.

Code Example 4-1   Continuation Semantics

```
unsigned int nestcount;

unsigned int A(int i, int j) {
    nestcount++;

    if (i==0)
        return(j+1)
    else if (j==0)
        return(A(i-1, 1));
    else
        return(A(i-1, A(i, j-1)));
}

void sig(int i) {
    printf("nestcount = %d\n", nestcount);
}

main() {
    sigset(SIGINT, sig);
    A(4,4);
}
```

New Operations on Signals

Several new signal operations for multithreaded programming have been added to the operating system.

thr_sigsetmask(3T)

`thr_sigsetmask(3T)` does for a thread what `sigprocmask(2)` does for a process—it sets the (thread's) signal mask. When a new thread is created, its initial mask is inherited from its creator.

Avoid using `sigprocmask()` in multithreaded programs because it sets the signal mask of the underlying LWP, and the thread that is affected by this can change over time.

Unlike `sigprocmask()`, `thr_sigsetmask()` is relatively inexpensive to call because it does not generally cause a system call, as does `sigprocmask()`.

thr_kill(3T)

`thr_kill(3T)` is the thread analog of `kill(2)`—it sends a signal to a specific thread.

This, of course, is different from sending a signal to a process. When a signal is sent to a process, the signal can be handled by any thread in the process. A signal sent by `thr_kill()` can be handled only by the specified thread.

Note than you can use `thr_kill()` to send signals only to threads in the current process. This is because the thread identifier (type `thread_t`) is local in scope—it is not possible to name a thread in any process but your own.

sigwait(2)

`sigwait(2)` causes the calling thread to wait until any signal identified by its *set* argument is delivered to the thread. While the thread is waiting, signals identified by the *set* argument are unmasked, but the original mask is restored when the call returns.

Use `sigwait()` to separate threads from asynchronous signals. You can create one thread that is listening for asynchronous signals while your other threads are created to block any asynchronous signals that might be set to this process.

When the signal is delivered, `sigwait()` clears the pending signal and returns its number. Many threads can call `sigwait()` at the same time, but only one thread returns for each signal that is received.

With `sigwait()` you can treat asynchronous signals synchronously—a thread that deals with such signals simply calls `sigwait()` and returns as soon as a signal arrives. By ensuring that all threads (including the caller of `sigwait()`) have such signals masked, you can be sure that signals are handled only by the intended handler and that they are handled safely.

Usually, you use `sigwait()` to create one or more threads that wait for signals. Because `sigwait()` can retrieve even masked signals, be sure to block the signals of interest in all other threads so they are not accidentally delivered. When the signals arrive, a thread returns from `sigwait()`, handles the signal, and waits for more signals. The signal-handling thread is not restricted to using Async-Safe functions and can synchronize with other threads in the usual way. (The Async-Safe category is defined in "MT Interface Safety Levels" on page 95.)

Note – `sigwait()` should *never* be used with synchronous signals.

---

sigtimedwait(2)

sigtimedwait(2) is similar to sigwait(2) except that it fails and returns an error when a signal is not received in the indicated amount of time.

Thread-Directed Signals

The UNIX signal mechanism is extended with the idea of *thread-directed signals*. These are just like ordinary asynchronous signals, except that they are sent to a particular thread instead of to a process.

Waiting for asynchronous signals in a separate thread can be safer and easier than installing a signal handler and processing the signals there.

A better way to deal with asynchronous signals is to treat them synchronously. By calling sigwait(2), discussed on page 82, a thread can wait until a signal occurs.

Code Example 4-2   Asynchronous Signals and sigwait(2)

```
main() {
    sigset_t set;
    void runA(void);

    sigemptyset(&set);
    sigaddset(&set, SIGINT);
    thr_sigsetmask(SIG_BLOCK, &set, NULL);
    thr_create(NULL, 0, runA, NULL, THR_DETACHED, NULL);

    while (1) {
        sigwait(&set);
        printf("nestcount = %d\n", nestcount);
    }
}

void runA() {
    A(4,4);
    exit(0);
}
```

Code Example 4-2 modifies the code of Code Example 4-1: the main routine masks the SIGINT signal, creates a child thread that calls the function *A* of the previous example, and finally issues sigwaits to handle the SIGINT signal.

Note that the signal is masked in the compute thread because the compute thread inherits its signal mask from the main thread. The main thread is protected from SIGINT while, and only while, it is not blocked inside of sigwait().

Also, note that there is never any danger of having system calls interrupted when you use sigwait().

Completion Semantics

Another way to deal with signals is with *completion semantics*. Use completion semantics when a signal indicates that something so catastrophic has happened that there is no reason to continue executing the current code block. The signal handler runs *instead of* the remainder of the block that had the problem. In other words, the signal handler *completes* the block.

In Code Example 4-3, the block in question is the body of the then part of the if statement. The call to setjmp(3C) saves the current register state of the program in jbuf and returns 0—thereby executing the block.

Code Example 4-3   Completion Semantics

```
sigjmp_buf jbuf;
void mult_divide(void) {
    int a, b, c, d;
    void problem();

    sigset(SIGFPE, problem);
    while (1) {
        if (sigsetjmp(&jbuf) == 0) {
            printf("Three numbers, please:\n");
            scanf("%d %d %d", &a, &b, &c);
            d = a*b/c;
            printf("%d*%d/%d = %d\n", a, b, c, d);
        }
    }
}

void problem(int sig) {
    printf("Couldn't deal with them, try again\n");
    siglongjmp(&jbuf, 1);
}
```

If a SIGFPE (a floating-point exception) occurs, the signal handler is invoked.

The signal handler calls siglongjmp(3C), which restores the register state saved in jbuf, causing the program to return from sigsetjmp() again (among the registers saved are the program counter and the stack pointer).

This time, however, sigsetjmp(3C) returns the second argument of siglongjmp(), which is 1. Notice that the block is skipped over, only to be executed during the next iteration of the while loop.

Note that you can use sigsetjmp(3C) and siglongjmp(3C) in multithreaded programs, but be careful that a thread never does a siglongjmp() using the results of another thread's sigsetjmp(). Also, sigsetjmp() and siglongjmp() save and restore the signal mask, but setjmp(3C) and longjmp(3C) do not. It is best to use sigsetjmp() and siglongjmp() when you work with signal handlers.

Completion semantics are often used to deal with exceptions. In particular, the Ada® programming language uses this model.

Note – Remember, sigwait(2) should *never* be used with synchronous signals.

Signal Handlers and Async Safety

A concept similar to thread safety is *async safety*. Async-Safe operations are guaranteed not to interfere with operations being interrupted.

The problem of async safety arises when the actions of a signal handler can interfere with the operation being interrupted. For example, suppose a program is in the middle of a call to printf(3S) and a signal occurs whose handler itself calls printf(): the output of the two printf() statements would be intertwined. To avoid this, the handler should not call printf() itself when printf() might be interrupted by a signal.

This problem cannot be solved by using synchronization primitives because any attempted synchronization between the signal handler and the operation being synchronized would produce immediate deadlock.

For example, suppose that printf() is to protect itself by using a mutex. Now suppose that a thread that is in a call to printf(), and so holds the lock on the mutex, is interrupted by a signal. If the handler (being called by the thread that is still inside of printf()) itself calls printf(), the thread that holds the lock on the mutex will attempt to take it again, resulting in an instant deadlock.

To avoid interference between the handler and the operation, either ensure that the situation never arises (perhaps by masking off signals at critical moments) or invoke only Async-Safe operations from inside signal handlers.

Because setting a thread's mask is an inexpensive user-level operation, you can inexpensively make functions or sections of code fit in the Async-Safe category.

Interrupted Waits on Condition Variables

When a signal is delivered to a thread while the thread is waiting on a condition variable, the old convention (assuming that the process is not terminated) is that interrupted calls return EINTR.

The ideal new condition would be that when cond_wait(3T) and cond_timedwait(3T) return, the lock has been retaken on the mutex.

This is what is done in Solaris threads: when a thread is blocked in cond_wait() or cond_timedwait() and an unmasked, caught signal is delivered to the thread, the handler is invoked and the call to cond_wait() or cond_timedwait() returns EINTR with the mutex locked.

This implies that the mutex is locked in the signal handler because the handler might have to clean up after the thread.

This is illustrated by Code Example 4-4.

Code Example 4-4   Condition Variables and Interrupted Waits

```
int sig_catcher() {
    sigset_t set;
    void hdlr();

    mutex_lock(&mut);

    sigemptyset(&set);
    sigaddset(&set, SIGINT);
    thr_sigsetmask(SIG_UNBLOCK, &set, 0);

    if (cond_wait(&cond, &mut) == EINTR) {
        /* signal occurred and lock is held */
        cleanup();
        mutex_unlock(&mut);
        return(0);
    }
    normal_processing();
    mutex_unlock(&mut);
    return(1);
}

void hdlr() {
    /* lock is held in the handler */
    ...
}
```

Assume that the SIGINT signal is blocked in all threads on entry to sig_catcher() and that hdlr() has been established (with a call to sigaction(2)) as the handler for the SIGINT signal.

When an unmasked and caught instance of the SIGINT signal is delivered to the thread while it is in cond_wait(), the thread first reacquires the lock on the mutex, then calls hdlr(), and then returns EINTR from cond_wait().

Note that whether SA_RESTART has been specified as a flag to sigaction() has no effect here—cond_wait(3T) is not a system call and is not automatically restarted. When a caught signal occurs while a thread is blocked in cond_wait(), the call always returns EINTR.

4

I/O Issues

One of the attractions of multithreaded programming is I/O performance. The traditional UNIX API gave the programmer little assistance in this area—you either used the facilities of the file system or bypassed the file system entirely.

This section shows how to use threads to get more flexibility through I/O concurrency and multibuffering. This section also discusses the differences and similarities between the approaches of synchronous I/O (with threads) and asynchronous I/O (with and without threads).

I/O as a Remote Procedure Call

In the traditional UNIX model, I/O appears to be *synchronous*, as if you were placing a remote procedure call to the I/O device. Once the call returns, then the I/O has completed (or at least it appears to have completed—a write request, for example, might merely result in the transfer of the data to a buffer in the operating system).

The advantage of this model is that it is easy to understand because programmers are very familiar with the concept of procedure calls.

An alternative approach not found in traditional UNIX systems is the *asynchronous* model, in which an I/O request merely starts an operation. The program must somehow discover when the operation completes.

This approach is not as simple as the synchronous model, but it has the advantage of allowing concurrent I/O and processing in traditional, single-threaded UNIX processes.

Tamed Asynchrony

You can get most of the benefits of asynchronous I/O by using synchronous I/O in a multithreaded program. Where, with asynchronous I/O, you would issue a request and check later to determine when it completes, you can instead have a separate thread perform the I/O synchronously. The main thread can then check (perhaps by calling thr_join(3T)) for the completion of the operation at some later time.

Asynchronous I/O

In most situations there is no need for asynchronous I/O, since its effects can be achieved with the use of threads, each doing synchronous I/O. However, in a few situations, threads cannot achieve what asynchronous I/O can.

The most straightforward example is writing to a tape drive to make the tape drive *stream*. This technique prevents the tape drive from stopping while it is being written to and moves the tape forward at high speed while supplying a constant stream of data that it writes to tape.

To do this, the tape driver in the kernel must issue a queued write request when the tape driver responds to an interrupt indicating that the previous tape-write operation has completed.

Threads cannot guarantee that asynchronous writes will be ordered because the order in which threads execute is indeterminate. Trying to order a write to a tape, for example, is not possible.

Asynchronous I/O Operations

```
#include <sys/asynch.h>

int aioread(int fildes, char *bufp, int bufs, off_t offset,
    int whence, aio_result_t *resultp);

int aiowrite(int filedes, const char *bufp, int bufs,
    off_t offset, int whence, aio_result_t *resultp);

aio_result_t *aiowait(const struct timeval *timeout);

int aiocancel(aio_result_t *resultp);
```

aioread(3) and aiowrite(3) are similar in form to pread(2) and pwrite(2), except for the addition of the last argument. Calls to aioread() and aiowrite() result in the initiation (or queueing) of an I/O operation.

The call returns without blocking, and the status of the call is returned in the structure pointed to by resultp. This is an item of type aio_result_t that contains

```
int aio_return;
int aio_errno;
```

When a call fails immediately, the failure code can be found in aio_errno. Otherwise, this field contains AIO_INPROGRESS, meaning that the operation has been successfully queued.

You can wait for an outstanding asynchronous I/O operation to complete by calling aiowait(3). This returns a pointer to the aio_result_t structure supplied with the original aioread(3) or aiowrite(3) call. This time aio_result contains whatever read(2) or write(2) would have returned if it had been called instead of the asynchronous versions, and aio_errno contains the error code, if any.

aiowait() takes a timeout argument, which indicates how long the caller is willing to wait. As usual, a NULL pointer here means that the caller is willing to wait indefinitely, and a pointer to a structure containing a zero value means that the caller is unwilling to wait at all.

You might start an asynchronous I/O operation, do some work, then call aiowait() to wait for the request to complete. Or you can use SIGIO to be notified, asynchronously, when the operation completes.

Finally, a pending asynchronous I/O operation can be cancelled by calling aiocancel(). This routine is called with the address of the result area as an argument. This result area identifies which operation is being cancelled.

Shared I/O and New I/O System Calls

When multiple threads are performing I/O operations at the same time with the same file descriptor, you might discover that the traditional UNIX I/O interface is not thread-safe. The problem occurs with non-sequential I/O. This uses the lseek(2) system call to set the file offset, which is then used in the next read(2) or write(2) call to indicate where in the file the operation should start. When two or more threads are issuing lseek(2)'s to the same file descriptor, a conflict results.

To avoid this conflict, use the new pread(2) and pwrite(2) system calls.

```
#include <sys/types.h>
#include <unistd.h>

ssize_t pread(int fildes, void *buf, size_t nbyte, off_t offset);

ssize_t pwrite(int filedes, void *buf, size_t nbyte,
    off_t offset);
```

These behave just like read(2) and write(2) except that they take an additional argument, the *file offset*. With this argument, you specify the offset without using lseek(2), so multiple threads can use these routines safely for I/O on the same file descriptor.

Alternatives to getc(3S) and putc(3S)

An additional problem occurs with standard I/O. Programmers are accustomed to routines such as getc(3S) and putc(3S) being very quick—they are implemented as macros. Because of this, they can be used within the inner loop of a program with no concerns about efficiency.

However, when they are made thread safe they suddenly become more expensive—they now require (at least) two internal subroutine calls, to lock and unlock a mutex. To get around this problem, alternative versions of these routines are supplied—getc_unlocked(3S) and putc_unlocked(3S).

These do not acquire locks on a mutex and so are as quick as the originals, nonthread-safe versions of getc(3S) and putc(3S). However, to use them in a thread-safe way, you must explicitly lock and release the mutexes that protect the standard I/O streams, using flockfile(3S) and funlockfile(3S). The calls to these latter routines are placed outside the loop, and the calls to getc_unlocked() or putc_unlocked() are placed inside the loop.

4

Multithreaded Programming Guide

Safe and Unsafe Interfaces 5 ≡

This chapter defines MT-safety levels for functions and libraries.

Thread Safety

Thread safety is the avoidance of *data races*—situations in which data are set to either correct or incorrect values depending upon the order in which multiple threads access and modify the data.

When no sharing is intended, give each thread a private copy of the data. When sharing is important, provide explicit synchronization to make certain that the program behaves deterministically.

A procedure is *thread safe* when it is logically correct when executed simultaneously by several threads. At a practical level, it is convenient to recognize three levels of safety.

- Unsafe
- Thread safe – Serializable
- Thread safe – MT-safe

An unsafe procedure can be made serializable by surrounding it with statements locking and unlocking a mutex. Code Example 5-1 on page 94 shows first a nonthread-safe implementation of a simplified fputs().

Next is a serializable version of this routine with a single mutex protecting the procedure from concurrent execution problems. Actually, this is stronger synchronization than is necessary in this case. When two threads are calling fputs() to print to different files, one need not wait for the other—both can safely print at the same time.

The last version of the routine is *MT-safe*. It uses one lock for each file, allowing two threads to print to different files at the same time. So, a routine is *MT-safe* when it is thread safe and its execution does not negatively affect performance.

Code Example 5-1   Degrees of Thread Safety

```
/* not thread-safe */
fputs(const char *s, FILE *stream) {
    char *p;
    for (p=s; *p; p++)
        putc((int)*p, stream);
    }

/* serializable */
fputs(const char *s, FILE *stream) {
    static mutex_t mut;
    char *p;
    mutex_lock(&m);
    for (p=s; *p; p++)
        putc((int)*p, stream);

    mutex_unlock(&m);
}

/* MT-Safe */
mutex_t m[NFILE];
fputs(const char *s, FILE *stream) {
    static mutex_t mut;
    char *p;
    mutex_lock(&m[fileno(stream)]);
    for (p=s; *p; p++)
        putc((int)*p, stream);
    mutex_unlock(&m[fileno(stream)]0;
}
```

MT Interface Safety Levels

The *man Pages(3): Library Routines* use the categories listed in Table 5-1 to describe how well an interface supports threads (these categories are explained more fully in the Intro(3) man page).

Table 5-1   Categories Used by Library Routines

Category	Description
Safe	This code can be called from a multithreaded application.
Safe with exceptions	See the NOTES sections of these pages for a description of the exceptions.
Unsafe	This interface is not safe to use with multithreaded applications unless the application arranges for only one thread at a time to execute within the library.
MT-Safe	This interface is fully prepared for multithreaded access in that it is both *safe* and it supports some concurrency.
MT-Safe with exceptions	See the NOTES sections of these pages in the *man Pages(3): Library Routines* for descriptions of the exceptions.
Async-Safe	This routine can safely be called from a signal handler. A thread that is executing an Async-Safe routine does not deadlock with itself when interrupted by a signal.

See the table in Appendix B, "MT Safety Levels: Library Interfaces," for a list of *safe* interfaces from the *man Pages(3): Library Routines*. If an interface from Section 3 is not in this table, it is probably unsafe (this does not include the Source Compatibility Library). Check the man page to be sure.

All functions described in the *man Pages(2): System Calls* are MT-Safe except for vfork(2).

Some functions have purposely not been made safe for the following reasons.

- Making the function MT-Safe would have negatively affected the performance of single-threaded applications.

- The function has an Unsafe interface. For example, a function might return a pointer to a buffer in the stack. You can use reentrant counterparts for some of these functions. The reentrant function name is the original function name with "_r" appended.

 Caution – There is no way to be certain that a function whose name does not end in "_r" is MT-Safe other than by checking its reference manual page. Use of a function identified as not MT-Safe must be protected by a synchronizing device or restricted to the initial thread.

Reentrant Functions for Unsafe Interfaces

For most functions with Unsafe interfaces, an MT-Safe version of the routine exists. The name of the new MT-Safe routine is always the name of the old Unsafe routine with "_r" appended. The "_r" routines listed in Table 5-2 are supplied in the Solaris system:

Table 5-2   Reentrant Functions

asctime_r(3C)	ctermid_r(3S)	ctime_r(3C)
fgetgrent_r(3C)	fgetpwent_r(3C)	fgetspent_r(3C)
gamma_r(3M)	getgrgid_r(3C)	getgrnam_r(3C)
getlogin_r(3C)	getpwnam_r(3C)	getpwuid_r(3C)
getgrent_r(3C)	gethostbyaddr_r(3N)	gethostbyname_r(3N)
gethostent_r(3N)	getnetbyaddr_r(3N)	getnetbyname_r(3N)
getnetent_r(3N)	getprotobyname_r(3N)	getprotobynumber_r(3N)
getprotoent_r(3N)	getpwent_r(3C)	getrpcbyname_r(3N)
getrpcbynumber_r(3N)	getrpcent_r(3N)	getservbyname_r(3N)
getservbyport_r(3N)	getservent_r(3N)	getspent_r(3C)
getspnam_r(3C)	gmtime_r(3C)	lgamma_r(3M)
localtime_(3C)r	nis_sperror_r(3N)	rand_r(3C)
readdir_r(3C)	strtok_r(3C)	tmpnam_r(3C)
ttyname_r(3C)		

Async-Safe Functions

Functions that can safely be called from signal handlers are *Async-Safe*. The POSIX standard defines and lists Async-Safe functions (IEEE Std 1003.1-1990, 3.3.1.3 (3)(f), page 55). In addition to the POSIX Async-Safe functions, the following three functions from the threads library are also async safe.

- sema_post(3T)
- thr_sigsetmask(3T)
- thr_kill(3T)

MT Safety Levels for Libraries

All routines that can potentially be called by a thread from a multithreaded program should be MT-Safe.

This means that two or more activations of a routine must be able to *correctly* execute concurrently. So, every library interface that a multithreaded program uses must be MT-Safe.

Not all libraries are now MT-Safe. The commonly used libraries that are MT-Safe are listed in Table 5-3. Additional libraries will eventually be modified to be MT-Safe.

Table 5-3   Some MT-Safe Libraries

Library	Comments
lib/libc	get*XX*by*YY* interfaces are MT-Safe
lib/libdl_stubs	(To support static switch compiling)
lib/libintl	
lib/libm	MT-Safe only when compiled for the shared library, but not MT-Safe when linked with the archived library
lib/libmalloc	
lib/libmapmalloc	
lib/libnsl	Including the TLI interface, XDR, RPC clients and servers, `netdir`, and `netselect`. get*XX*by*YY* interfaces are not safe, but have thread-safe interfaces of the form getXXbyYY_r
lib/libresolv	(Thread-specific errno support)
lib/libsocket	
lib/libw	
lib/nametoaddr	
libX11	
libC	(Not part of the Solaris system; can be purchased separately).

Unsafe Libraries

Routines in libraries that are not guaranteed to be MT-Safe can safely be called by multithreaded programs only when such calls are single-threaded.

Compiling and Debugging 6

This chapter describes how to compile and debug your multithreaded programs.

Compiling a Multithreaded Application

Using the C Compiler

Make sure the following software is available so you can successfully compile and link a multithreaded program.

- Include files:
  - `thread.h`
  - `errno.h`

- The standard C compiler

- The standard Solaris linker

- The threads library (`libthread`)

- MT-safe libraries (`libc`, `libm`, `libw`, `libintl`, `libmalloc`, `libmapmalloc`, `libnsl`, and so on)

Compiling with the _REENTRANT Flag

Compile multithread programs with the `-D _REENTRANT` flag.

This applies to every module of a new application. When the `-D_REENTRANT` flag is not present, the old definitions for `errno`, `stdio`, and so on, are used. To compile a single-threaded application, make sure that the `_REENTRANT` flag is undefined.

Link Old with New Carefully

Table 6-1 shows that multithreaded object modules should be linked with old object modules only with great caution.

Table 6-1   Compiling with and without the _REENTRANT Flag

The File Type	Compiled	Reference	And Return
Old object files (nonthreaded) and new object files	*Without* the _REENTRANT flag	Static storage	The traditional errno
New object files	*With* the _REENTRANT flag	__errno, the new binary entry point	The address of the thread's definition of errno
Programs using TLI in libnsl[1]	*With* the _REENTRANT flag (required)	__t_errno, a new entry point	The address of the thread's definition of t_errno

1. Include tiuser.h to get the TLI global error variable.

Using libthread

To use libthread, specify –lthread before –lc on the ld command line, or last on the cc command line.

All calls to libthread are no-ops if the application does not link libthread.

libc has defined libthread stubs that are null procedures. True procedures are interposed by libthread when the application links both libc and libthread.

The behavior of the C library is undefined if a program is constructed with an ld command line that includes the fragment:

```
.o's ... -lc -lthread ...
```

Do not link a single-threaded program with -lthread. Doing so establishes multithreading mechanisms at link time that are initiated at run time. These waste resources and produce misleading results when you debug your code.

Using Non-C Compilers

The threads library uses the following items from libc:

- System call wrappers
- Something (usually printf()) to display error messages
- Runtime linking support to resolve symbols (because the library is dynamically linked)

You can eliminate these dependencies by writing both your own system call wrappers and your own printf() function, and by having the linker resolve all libthread symbols at link time rather than at runtime.

The threads library does not use dynamically allocated memory when the threads are created with application-supplied stacks. The thr_create(3T) routine lets the application specify its own stacks.

Debugging Multithreaded Programs

Common Oversights

The following list points out some of the more frequent oversights that can cause bugs in multithreaded programming.

- Using a local or global variable for passing an argument to a new thread

- Accessing global memory (shared changeable state) without the protection of a synchronization mechanism

- Creating deadlocks caused by two threads trying to acquire rights to the same pair of global resources in alternate order (so that one thread controls the first resource and the other controls the second resource and neither can proceed until the other gives up)

- Creating a hidden gap in synchronization protection. This is caused when a code segment protected by a synchronization mechanism contains a call to a function that frees and then reacquires the synchronization mechanism before it returns to the caller. The result is that it appears to the caller that the global data has been protected when it actually has not.

- Making deeply nested, recursive calls and using large automatic arrays can cause problems because multithreaded programs have a more limited stack size than single-threaded programs.

- Specifying an inadequate stack size

- Providing stack other than through the thread library calls

And, note that multithreaded programs (especially buggy ones) often behave differently in two successive runs given identical inputs because of differences in the thread scheduling order.

In general, multithreading bugs are statistical instead of deterministic in character. Tracing is usually more effective in finding problems in the order of execution than is breakpoint-based debugging.

Using adb

When you bind all threads in a multithreaded program, a thread and an LWP are synonymous. Then you can access each thread with the adb commands (described in Table 6-2) that support multithreaded programming.

Table 6-2   MT adb commands

Command	Description
pid:A	Attaches to process # *pid*. This stops the process and all its LWPs.
:R	Detaches from process. This resumes the process and all its LWPs.
$L	Lists all active LWPs in the (stopped) process.
n:l	Switches focus to LWP # *n*
$l	Shows the LWP currently focused
num:i	Ignores signal number *num*

Using dbx

With the dbx utility you can debug and execute source programs written in C++, ANSI C, FORTRAN, and Pascal. dbx accepts the same commands as the SPARCworks™ Debugger but uses a standard terminal (tty) interface. Both dbx and the SPARCworks Debugger now support debugging multithreaded programs.

For a full overview of dbx and Debugger features see the SunPro dbx(1) man page and the *Debugging a Program* user's guide.

The dbx options listed in Table 6-3 support multithreaded programs.

Table 6-3   dbx Options for MT Programs

Option	Description
cont at *line* [*sig signo id*]	Continues execution at line *line* with signal *signo*. See continue for dbx command language loop control. The *id*, if present, specifies which thread or LWP to continue. Default value is *all*.
lwp	Displays current LWP. Switches to given LWP [lwpid].
lwps	Lists all LWPs in the current process.
next ... tid	Steps the given thread. When a function call is skipped, all LWPs are implicitly resumed for the duration of that function call. Nonactive threads cannot be stepped.
next ... lid	Steps the given LWP. Does not implicitly resume all LWPs when skipping a function. The LWP on which the given thread is active. Does not implicitly resume all LWP when skipping a function.

Table 6-3   dbx Options for MT Programs (Continued)

Option	Description
step... tid	Steps the given thread. When a function call is skipped, all LWPs are implicitly resumed for the duration of that function call. Nonactive threads cannot be stepped.
step... lid	Steps the given LWP. Does not implicitly resume all LWPs when skipping a function.
stepi... lid	The given LWP.
stepi... tid	The LWP on which the given thread is active.
thread	Displays current thread. Switches to thread *tid*. In all the following variations, an optional *tid* implies the current thread.
thread -info [tid]	Prints everything known about the given thread.
thread -locks [tid]	Prints all locks held by the given thread.
thread -suspend [tid]	Puts the given thread into suspended state.
thread -continue [tid]	Unsuspends the given thread.
thread -hide [tid]	*Hide*s the given (or current) thread. It will not show up in the generic threads listing.
thread -unhide [tid]	*Unhide*s the given (or current) thread.
allthread-unhide	*Unhide*s all threads.
threads	Prints the list of all known threads.
threads-all	Prints threads that are not usually printed (zombies).
all	filterthreads-mode	Controls whether threads prints all threads or filters them by default.
auto	manualthreads-mode	Enables automatic updating of the thread listing in the Thread Inspector of the GUI interface (SPARCworks Debugger).
threads-mode	Echoes the current modes. Any of the previous forms can be followed by a thread or LWP ID to get the traceback for the specified entity.

Programming Guidelines 7 ≡

This chapter gives some pointers on programming with threads. Differences between single-threaded thinking and multithreaded thinking are emphasized.

Historically, most code has been designed for single-threaded programs. This is especially true for most of the library routines called from C programs. The following implicit assumptions were made for single-threaded code:

- When you write into a global variable and then, a moment later, read from it, what you read is exactly what you just wrote.

- This is also true for non-global, static storage.

- You do not need synchronization because there is nothing to synchronize with.

The next few examples discuss some of the problems that arise in multithreaded programs because of these assumptions, and how you can deal with them.

Rethinking Global Variables

Traditional, single-threaded C and UNIX have a convention for handling errors detected in system calls. System calls can return anything as a functional value (for example, write() returns the number of bytes that were transferred). However, the value -1 is reserved to indicate that something went wrong. So, when a system call returns -1, you know that it failed.

Code Example 7-1   Global Variables and errno

```
extern int errno;
...
if (write(file_desc, buffer, size) == -1) {
    /* the system call failed */
    fprintf(stderr, "something went wrong, "
        "error code = %d\n", errno);
    exit(1);
}
...
```

Rather than return the actual error code (which could be confused with normal return values), the error code is placed into the global variable errno. When the system call fails, you can look in errno to find what went wrong.

Now consider what happens in a multithreaded environment when two threads fail at about the same time, but with different errors. Both expect to find their error codes in errno, but one copy of errno cannot hold both values. This global variable approach simply does not work for multithreaded programs.

The Solaris threads package solves this problem through a conceptually new storage class—thread-specific data. This storage is similar to global storage in that it can be accessed from any procedure in which a thread might be running. However, it is private to the thread—when two threads refer to the thread-specific data location of the same name, they are referring to two different areas of storage.

So, when using threads, each reference to errno is thread specific because each thread has a private copy of errno.

Providing For Static Local Variables

Code Example 7-2 shows a problem similar to the errno problem, but involving static storage instead of global storage. The function gethostbyname(3N) is called with the computer name as its argument. The return value is a pointer to a structure containing the required information for contacting the computer through network communications.

Code Example 7-2   The gethostbyname() Problem

```
struct hostent *gethostbyname(char *name) {
    static struct hostent result;
        /* Lookup name in hosts database */
        /* Put answer in result */
    return(&result);
}
```

Returning a pointer to an automatic local variable is generally not a good idea, although it works in this case because the variable is static. However, when two threads call this variable at once with different computer names, the use of static storage conflicts.

Thread-specific data could be used on a replacement for static storage, as in the errno problem, but this involves dynamic allocation of storage and adds to the expense of the call.

A better way to handle this kind of problem is to make the caller of gethostbyname() supply the storage for the result of the call. This is done by having the caller supply an additional argument, an output argument, to the routine. This requires a new interface to gethostbyname().

This technique is used in Solaris threads to fix many of these problems. In most cases, the name of the new interface is the old name with "_r" appended, as in gethostbyname_r(3N).

Synchronizing Threads

The threads in an application must cooperate and synchronize when sharing the data and the resources of the process.

A problem arises when multiple threads call something that manipulates an object. In a single-threaded world, synchronizing access to such objects is not a problem, but as Code Example 7-3 illustrates, this is a concern with multithreaded code. (Note that the Solaris printf(3S) is safe to call for a multithreaded program; this example illustrates what could happen if printf() were not safe.)

Code Example 7-3   The printf() Problem

```
/* thread 1: */
    printf("go to statement reached");


/* thread 2: */
    printf("hello world");



printed on display:
    go to hello
```

Single-Threaded Strategy

One strategy is to have a single, application-wide mutex lock that is acquired whenever any thread in the application is running and is released before it must block. Since only one thread can be accessing shared data at any one time, each thread has a consistent view of memory.

Because this is effectively a single-threaded program, very little is gained by this strategy.

Reentrance

A better approach is to take advantage of the principles of modularity and data encapsulation. A reentrant function is one that behaves correctly if it is called simultaneously by several threads. Writing a reentrant function is a matter of understanding just what *behaves correctly* means for this particular function.

Functions that are callable by several threads must be made reentrant. This might require changes to the function interface or to the implementation.

Functions that access global state, like memory or files, have reentrance problems. These functions need to protect their use of global state with the appropriate synchronization mechanisms provided by Solaris threads.

The two basic strategies for making functions in modules reentrant are code locking and data locking.

Code Locking

Code locking is done at the function call level and guarantees that a function executes entirely under the protection of a lock. The assumption is that all access to data is done through functions. Functions that share data should execute under the same lock.

Some parallel programming languages provide a construct called a monitor that implicitly does code locking for functions that are defined within the scope of the monitor. A monitor can also be implemented by a mutex lock.

Functions under the protection of the same mutex lock or within the same monitor are guaranteed to execute atomically with respect to each other.

Data Locking

Data locking guarantees that access to a *collection* of data is maintained consistently. For data locking, the concept of locking code is still there, but code locking is around references to shared (global) data, only. For a mutual exclusion locking protocol, only one thread can be in the critical section for each collection of data.

Alternatively, in a multiple readers, single writer protocol, several readers can be allowed for each collection of data or one writer. Multiple threads can execute in a single module when they operate on different data collections and do not conflict on a single collection for the multiple readers, single writer protocol. So, data locking typically allows more concurrency than does code locking.

What strategy should you use when using locks (whether implemented with mutexes, condition variables, or semaphores) in a program? Should you try to achieve maximum parallelism by locking only when necessary and unlocking as soon as possible (*fine-grained locking*)? Or should you hold locks for long periods to minimize the overhead of taking and releasing them (*coarse-grained locking*)?

The granularity of the lock depends on the amount of data it protects. A very coarse-grained lock might be a single lock to protect all data. Dividing how the data is protected by the appropriate number of locks is very important. Too fine a grain of locking can degrade performance. The small cost associated with acquiring and releasing locks can add up when there are too many locks.

The common wisdom is to start with a coarse-grained approach, identify bottlenecks, and add finer-grained locking where necessary to alleviate the bottlenecks. This is reasonably sound advice, but use your own judgment about taking it to the extreme.

Invariants

For both code locking and data locking, *invariants* are important to control locking complexity. An invariant is a condition or relation that is always true.

The definition is modified somewhat for concurrent execution: an invariant is a condition or relation that is true when the associated lock is being set. Once the lock is set, the invariant can be false. However, the code holding the lock must reestablish the invariant before releasing the lock.

An invariant can also be a condition or relation that is true when a lock is being set. Conditional variables can be thought of as having an invariant that is the condition.

Code Example 7-4   Testing the Invariant With assert(3X)

```
    mutex_lock(&lock);
    while(condition)
        cond_wait(&cv, &lock);
    assert((condition)==TRUE);
        .
        .
        .
    mutex_unlock();
```

The assert() statement is testing the invariant. The cond_wait() function does not preserve the invariant, which is why the invariant must be re-evaluated when the thread returns.

Another example is a module that manages a doubly linked list of elements. For each item on the list a good invariant is the forward pointer of the previous item on the list that should also point to the same thing as the backward pointer of the forward item.

Assume this module uses code-based locking and therefore is protected by a single global mutex lock. When an item is deleted or added the mutex lock is acquired, the correct manipulation of the pointers is made, and the mutex lock is released. Obviously, at some point in the manipulation of the pointers the invariant is false, but the invariant is reestablished before the mutex lock is released.

Avoiding Deadlock

Deadlock is a permanent blocking of a set of threads that are competing for a set of resources. Just because some thread can make progress does not mean that there is not a deadlock somewhere else.

The most common error causing deadlock is *self deadlock* or *recursive deadlock*: a thread tries to acquire a lock it is already holding. Recursive deadlock is very easy to program by mistake.

For example, if a code monitor has every module function grabbing the mutex lock for the duration of the call, then any call between the functions within the module protected by the mutex lock immediately deadlocks. If a function calls some code outside the module which, through some circuitous path, calls back into any method protected by the same mutex lock, then it will deadlock too.

The solution for this kind of deadlock is to avoid calling functions outside the module when you don't know whether they will call back into the module without reestablishing invariants and dropping all module locks before making the call. Of course, after the call completes and the locks are reacquired, the state must be verified to be sure the intended operation is still valid.

An example of another kind of deadlock is when two threads, thread 1 and thread 2, each acquires a mutex lock, A and B, respectively. Suppose that thread 1 tries to acquire mutex lock B and thread 2 tries to acquire mutex lock A. Thread 1 cannot proceed and it is blocked waiting for mutex lock B. Thread 2 cannot proceed and it is blocked waiting for mutex lock A. Nothing can change, so this is a permanent blocking of the threads, and a deadlock.

This kind of deadlock is avoided by establishing an order in which locks are acquired (a *lock hierarchy*). When all threads always acquire locks in the specified order, this deadlock is avoided.

Adhering to a strict order of lock acquisition is not always optimal. When thread 2 has many assumptions about the state of the module while holding mutex lock B, giving up mutex lock B to acquire mutex lock A and then reacquiring mutex lock B in order would cause it to discard its assumptions and reevaluate the state of the module.

The blocking synchronization primitives usually have variants that attempt to get a lock and fail if they cannot, such as `mutex_trylock()`. This allows threads to violate the lock hierarchy when there is no contention. When there is contention, the held locks must usually be discarded and the locks reacquired in order.

Scheduling Deadlocks

Because there is no guaranteed order in which locks are acquired, a common problem in threaded programs is that a particular thread never acquires a lock (usually a condition variable), even though it seems that it should.

This usually happens when the thread that holds the lock releases it, lets a small amount of time pass, and then reacquires it. Because the lock was released, it might seem that the other thread should acquire the lock. But, because nothing blocks the thread holding the lock, it continues to run from the time it releases the lock until it reacquires the lock, and so no other thread is run.

You can usually solve this type of problem by calling thr_yield(3T) just before the call to reacquire the lock. This allows other threads to run and to acquire the lock.

Because the time-slice requirements of applications are so variable, the threads library does not impose any. Use calls to thr_yield() to make threads share time as you require.

Locking Guidelines

Here are some simple guidelines for locking:

- Try not to hold locks across long operations like I/O where performance can be adversely affected.

- Don't hold locks when calling a function that is outside the module and that might reenter the module.

- Don't try for excessive processor concurrency. Without intervening system calls or I/O operation, locks are usually held for short amounts of time and contention is rare. Fix only those locks that have measured contention.

- When using multiple locks, avoid deadlocks by making sure that all threads acquire the locks in the same order.

Following Some Basic Guidelines

- Know what you are importing and whether it is safe.
  A threaded program cannot arbitrarily enter nonthreaded code.

- Threaded code can safely refer to unsafe code only from the initial thread.
  This ensures that the static storage associated with the initial thread is used only by that thread.

- Sun-supplied libraries are defined to be *safe* unless explicitly documented as unsafe.
  If a reference manual entry does not say whether a function is MT-Safe, it is safe. All MT-unsafe functions are identified explicitly in the manual page.

- Use compilation flags to manage binary incompatible source changes.
  Either specify -D_REENTRANT when compiling or be sure that _REENTRANT is defined before any header file is included.

- When making a library safe for multithreaded use, do not thread global process operations.

  Do not change global operations (or actions with global side effects) to behave in a threaded manner. For example, if file I/O is changed to per-thread operation, threads cannot cooperate in accessing files.

  For thread-specific behavior, or *thread cognizant* behavior, use thread facilities. For example, when the termination of main() should terminate only the thread that is exiting main(), the end of main() should be:

  ```
  thr_exit();
  /*NOTREACHED*/
  ```

Creating Threads

The Solaris threads package caches the threads data structure, stacks, and LWPs so that the repetitive creation of unbound threads can be inexpensive.

Unbound thread creation is very inexpensive when compared to process creation or even to bound thread creation. In fact, the cost is similar to unbound thread synchronization when you include the context switches to stop one thread and start another.

So, creating and destroying threads as they are required is usually better than attempting to manage a pool of threads that wait for independent work.

A good example of this is an RPC server that creates a thread for each request and destroys it when the reply is delivered, instead of trying to maintain a pool of threads to service requests.

While thread creation is relatively inexpensive when compared to process creation, it is not inexpensive when compared to the cost of a few instructions. Create threads for processing that lasts at least a couple of thousand machine instructions.

Thread Concurrency

By default, Solaris threads attempts to adjust the system execution resources (LWPs) used to run unbound threads to match the real number of active threads. While the Solaris threads package cannot make perfect decisions, it at least ensures that the process continues to make progress.

When you have some idea of the number of unbound threads that should be simultaneously active (executing code or system calls), tell the library through thr_setconcurrency(3T).

For example:

- A database server that has a thread for each user should tell Solaris threads the expected number of simultaneously active users.

- A window server that has one thread for each client should tell Solaris threads the expected number of simultaneously active clients.

- A file copy program that has one reader thread and one writer thread should tell Solaris threads that the desired concurrency level is two.

Alternatively, the concurrency level can be incremented by one through the THR_NEW_LWP flag as each thread is created.

Include unbound threads blocked on inter-process (USYNC_PROCESS) synchronization variables as active when you compute thread concurrency. Exclude bound threads—they do not require concurrency support from Solaris threads because they are equivalent to LWPs.

Efficiency

A new thread is created with thr_create(3T) in less time than an existing thread can be restarted. This means that it is more efficient to create a new thread when one is needed and have it call thr_exit(3T) when it has completed its task than it would be to stockpile an idle thread and restart it.

Bound Threads

Bound threads are more expensive than unbound threads. Because bound threads can change the attributes of the underlying LWP, the LWPs are not cached when the bound threads exit. Instead, the operating system provides a new LWP when a bound thread is created and destroys it when the bound thread exits.

Use bound threads only when a thread needs resources that are available only through the underlying LWP, such as a virtual time interval timer or an alternate stack, or when the thread must be visible to the kernel to be scheduled with respect to all other active threads in the system, as in realtime scheduling.

Use unbound threads even when you expect all threads to be active simultaneously. This allows Solaris threads to efficiently cache LWP and thread resources so that thread creation and destruction are fast.

Thread Creation Guidelines

Here are some simple guidelines for using threads.

- Use threads for independent activities that must do a meaningful amount of work.

- Use threads to take advantage of CPU concurrency.

- Use bound threads only when absolutely necessary, that is, when some facility of the underlying LWP is required.

Use `thr_setconcurrency`(3T) to tell Solaris threads how many threads you expect to be simultaneously active.

Working with Multiprocessors

The Solaris threads package lets you take advantage of multiprocessors. In many cases, programmers must be concerned with whether the multithreaded application runs on a uniprocessor or a multiprocessor.

One such case involves the memory model of the multiprocessor. You cannot always assume that changes made to memory by one processor are immediately reflected in the other processors' views of that memory.

Another multiprocessor issue is efficient synchronization when threads must wait until all have reached a common point in their execution.

Note – The issues discussed here are not important when the threads synchronization primitives are *always* used to access shared memory locations.

The Underlying Architecture

When threads synchronize access to shared storage locations using the Solaris threads synchronization routines, the effect of running a program on a shared-memory multiprocessor is identical to the effect of running the program on a uniprocessor.

However, in many situations a programmer might be tempted to take advantage of the multiprocessor and use "tricks" to avoid the synchronization routines. As Code Example 7-5 on page 117 and Code Example 7-6 on page 119 show, such tricks can be dangerous.

Understanding the memory models supported by common multiprocessor architectures helps to understand the dangers.

The major multiprocessor components are:

- The *processors* themselves
- *Store buffers*, which connect the processors to their caches
- *Caches*, which hold the contents of recently accessed or modified storage locations
- *memory*, which is the primary storage (and is shared by all processors).

In the simple traditional model, the multiprocessor behaves as if the processors are connected directly to memory: when one processor stores into a location and another immediately loads from the same location, the second processor loads what was stored by the first. Caches can be used to speed the average memory access, and the desired semantics can be achieved when the caches are kept consistent with one another.

A problem with this simple approach is that the processor must often be delayed to make certain that the desired semantics are achieved. Many modern multiprocessors use various techniques to prevent such delays, which, unfortunately, change the semantics of the memory model. Two of these techniques and their effects are explained in the next two examples.

"Shared-Memory" Multiprocessors

Consider the purported solution to the producer/consumer problem shown in Code Example 7-5. Although this program works on current SPARC-based multiprocessors, it assumes that all multiprocessors have strongly ordered memory. This program is therefore not portable.

Code Example 7-5   The Producer/Consumer Problem – Shared Memory Multiprocessors

```
                    char buffer[BSIZE];
                    unsigned int in = 0;
                    unsigned int out = 0;

void                            char
producer(char item) {             consumer(void) {
                                    char item;

    do                              do
        ;/* nothing */                 ;/* nothing */
    while                           while
        (in - out == BSIZE);           (in - out == 0);

    buffer[in%BSIZE] = item;        item = buffer[out%BSIZE];
    in++;                           out++;
}                               }
```

When this program has exactly one producer and exactly one consumer and is run on a shared-memory multiprocessor, it appears to be correct. The difference between in and out is the number of items in the buffer. The producer waits (by repeatedly computing this difference) until there is room for a new item, and the consumer waits until there is an item in the buffer.

For memory that is *strongly ordered* (for instance, a modification to memory on one processor is immediately available to the other processors), this solution is correct (it is correct even taking into account that in and out will eventually overflow, as long as BSIZE is less than the largest integer that can be represented in a word).

Shared-memory multiprocessors do not necessarily have strongly ordered memory. A change to memory by one processor is not necessarily available immediately to the other processors. When two changes to different memory locations are made by one processor, the other processors do not necessarily see the changes in the order in which they were made because changes to memory don't happen immediately.

First the changes are stored in *store buffers* that are not visible to the cache. The processor looks at these store buffers to ensure that a program has a consistent view, but because store buffers are not visible to other processors, a write by one processor doesn't become visible until it is written to cache.

The Solaris synchronization primitives (see Chapter 3, "Programming with Synchronization Objects") use special instructions that flush the store buffers to cache. So, using locks around your shared data ensures memory consistency.

When memory ordering is very relaxed, Code Example 7-5 has a problem because the consumer might see that in has been incremented by the producer before it sees the change to the corresponding buffer slot. This is called *weak ordering* because stores made by one processor can appear to happen out of order by another processor (memory, however, is always consistent from the same processor). To fix this, the code should use mutexes to flush the cache.

The trend is toward relaxing memory order. Because of this, programmers are becoming increasingly careful to use locks around all global or shared data. As demonstrated by Code Example 7-5 and Code Example 7-6, locking is essential.

Peterson's Algorithm

The code in Code Example 7-6 is an implementation of Peterson's Algorithm, which handles mutual exclusion between two threads. This code tries to guarantee that there is never more than one thread in the critical section and that, when a thread calls mut_excl(), it enters the critical section sometime "soon."

An assumption here is that a thread exits fairly quickly after entering the critical section.

Code Example 7-6   Mutual Exclusion for Two Threads?

```
void mut_excl(int me /* 0 or 1 */) {
    static int loser;
    static int interested[2] = {0, 0};
    int other; /* local variable */

    other = 1 - me;
    interested[me] = 1;
    loser = me;
    while (loser == me && interested[other])
        ;

    /* critical section */
    interested[me] = 0;
}
```

This algorithm works some of the time when it is assumed that the multiprocessor has strongly ordered memory.

Some multiprocessors, including some SPARC-based multiprocessors, have store buffers. When a thread issues a store instruction, the data is put into a store buffer. The buffer contents are eventually sent to the cache, but not necessarily right away. (Note that the caches on each of the processors maintain a consistent view of memory, but modified data does not reach the cache right away.)

When multiple memory locations are stored into, the changes reach the cache (and memory) in the correct order, but possibly after a delay. SPARC-based multiprocessors with this property are said to have *total store order* (TSO).

When one processor stores into location *A* and then loads from location *B*, and another processor stores into location *B* and loads from location *A*, the expectation is that either the first processor fetches the newly modified value in location *B* or the second processor fetches the newly modified value in location *A*, or both, but that the case in which both processors load the old values simply cannot happen.

However, with the delays caused by load and store buffers, the "impossible case" can happen.

What could happen with Peterson's algorithm is that two threads running on separate processors each stores into its own slot of the interested array and then loads from the other slot. They both see the old values (0), assume that the other party is not present, and both enter the critical section. (Note that this is the sort of problem that might not show up when you test a program, but only much later.)

This problem is avoided when you use the threads synchronization primitives, whose implementations issue special instructions to force the writing of the store buffers to the cache.

Parallelizing a Loop on a Shared-Memory Parallel Computer

In many applications, and especially numerical applications, while part of the algorithm can be parallelized, other parts are inherently sequential (as shown in Code Example 7-7).

Code Example 7-7   Multithreaded Cooperation (Barrier Synchronization)

```
while(a_great_many_iterations) {

    sequential_computation

    parallel_computation
}
```

For example, you might produce a set of matrices with a strictly linear computation, then perform operations on the matrices using a parallel algorithm, then use the results of these operations to produce another set of matrices, then operate on them in parallel, and so on.

The nature of the parallel algorithms for such a computation is that little synchronization is required during the computation, but synchronization of all the threads employed is required at the end to ensure that all have finished.

When the time spent executing the parallel algorithm is large compared to the time required to create and synchronize the threads, the cost of thread creation and synchronization is no problem. But if the time required for the computation is not so large, then the thread-creation and synchronization times become very important.

Summary

This guide has covered basic threads programming issues. Look in Appendix A, "Sample Application Code" for program examples that use many of the features and styles that have been discussed.

Further Reading

For more information related to the subjects in this guide, see the following books:

- *Algorithms for Mutual Exclusion* by Michel Raynal (MIT Press, 1986)

- *Concurrent Programming* by Alan Burns & Geoff Davies (Addison-Wesley, 1993)

- *Distributed Algorithms and Protocols* by Michel Raynal (Wiley, 1988)

- *Operating System Concepts* by Silberschatz, Peterson, & Galvin (Addison-Wesley, 1991)

- *Principles of Concurrent Programming* by M. Ben-Ari (Prentice-Hall, 1982)

7

Sample Application Code

The following sample programs give you an idea of how to use multithreading in a variety of ways.

File Copy

Generating several I/O requests at once so that the I/O access time can be overlapped is often advantageous. A simple example of this is file copying. If the input and output files are on different devices, the read access for the next block can be overlapped with the write access for the last block. Code Example A-1 shows some of the code.

The main routine creates two threads: one to read the input, and one to write the output.

The reader thread reads from the input and places the data in a double buffer. The writer thread gets the data from the buffer and continuously writes it out. The threads synchronize using two counting semaphores; one that counts the number of buffers emptied by the writer and one that counts the number of buffers filled by the reader.

Note that the reader thread initializes semaphore emptybuf_sem because it needs a nonzero initial value. The writer thread need not explicitly initialize semaphore fullbuf_sem because it is allocated in zeroed memory.

Code Example A-1   File Copy Example With a Semaphore

```
sema_t emptybuf_sem, fullbuf_sem;

/* double buffer */
struct {
    char data[BSIZE];
```

Code Example A-1   File Copy Example With a Semaphore (Continued)

```
    int size;
} buf[2];

reader()
{
    int i = 0;

    sema_init(&emptybuf_sem, 2, 0, NULL);
    while (1) {
        sema_wait(&emptybuf_sem);
        buf[i].size = read(0, buf[i].data, BSIZE);
        sema_post(&fullbuf_sem);
        if (buf[i].size <= 0)
            break;
        i ^= 1;
    }
}

writer()
{
    int i = 0;

    while (1) {
        sema_wait(&fullbuf_sem);
        if (buf[i].size <= 0)
            break;

        write(1, buf[i].data, buf[i].size);
        sema_post(&emptybuf_sem);
        i ^= 1;
    }
}

main()
{
    thread_t twriter;

    (void)thr_create( NULL, NULL, reader, NULL, THR_DETACHED, NULL)
    (void)thr_create( NULL, NULL, writer, NULL, , &twriter, NULL);
    thr_join(twriter, NULL, NULL);
}
```

The example is a bit contrived because the system already generates asynchronous read-ahead and write-behind requests when accessing regular files. The example is still useful when the files to be copied are raw devices, since raw-device access is synchronous.

Matrix Multiplication

Computationally intensive applications benefit from the use of all available processors. Matrix multiplication is a good example of this.

When the matrix multiplication function is called, it acquires a mutex lock to ensure that only one matrix multiplication is in progress. This relies on mutex locks that are statically initialized to zero. The requesting thread checks whether its worker threads have been created. If not, it creates one for each CPU.

Once the worker threads are created, the requesting thread sets up a counter of work to do and signals the workers with a condition variable. Each worker selects a row and column from the input matrices, then updates the row and column variables so that the next worker will get the next row or column or both.

It then releases the mutex lock so that computing the vector product can proceed in parallel. When the results are ready, the worker reacquires the mutex lock and updates the counter of work completed. The worker that completes the last bit of work signals the requesting thread.

Code Example A-2   Matrix Multiplication

```
struct {
    mutex_t lock;
    cond_t start_cond, done_cond;
    int (*m1)[SZ][SZ], (*m2)[SZ][SZ], (*m3)[SZ][SZ];
    int row, col;
    int todo, notdone, workers;
} work;
mutex_t mul_lock;

void *
matmul(int (*m1)[SZ][SZ], int (*m2)[SZ][SZ], int (*m3)[SZ][SZ]);
{
    int i;

    mutex_lock(&mul_lock);
    mutex_lock(&work.lock);
```

Code Example A-2   Matrix Multiplication (Continued)

```
    if (work.workers == 0) {
        work.workers = sysconf (_SC_NPROCESSORS_ONLN);
        for (i = 0; i < work.workers; i++) {
            (void)thr_create (NULL, NULL, worker, (void *)NULL,
                         THR_NEW_LWP|THR_DETACHED, NULL);
        }
    }

    work.m1=m1; work.m2=m2; work.m3=m3;
    work.row = work.col = 0;
    work.todo = work.notdone = SZ*SZ;
    cond_broadcast(&work.start_cond);
    while (work.notdone)
        cond_wait(&work.done_cond, &work.lock);
    mutex_unlock(&work.lock);
    mutex_unlock(&mul_lock);
}
void *
worker()
{
    int (*m1)[SZ][SZ], (*m2)[SZ][SZ], (*m3)[SZ][SZ];
    int row, col, i, result;

    while (1) {
        mutex_lock(&work.lock);
        while (work.todo == 0)
            cond_wait(&work.start_cond, &work.lock);
        work.todo--;
        m1=work.m1; m2=work.m2; m3=work.m3;
        row = work.row; col = work.col;
        work.col++;
        if (work.col == SZ) {
            work.col = 0;
            work.row++;
            if (work.row == SZ)
                work.row = 0;
        }
        mutex_unlock(&work.lock);
        result = 0;
        for (i = 0; i < SZ; i++)
            result += (*m1)[row][i] * (*m2)[i][col];
        (*m3)[row][col] = result;
        mutex_lock(&work.lock);
```

Code Example A-2   Matrix Multiplication (Continued)

```
        work.notdone--;
        if (work.notdone == 0)
            cond_signal(&work.done_cond);
        mutex_unlock(&work.lock);
    }
}
```

Note that each iteration computed the results of one entry in the result matrix.

In some cases the amount of work is not sufficient to justify the overhead of synchronizing. In these cases it is better to give each worker more work per synchronization. For example, each worker could compute an entire row of the output matrix.

RPC Program

In a multithreaded client program, a thread can be created to issue each RPC request. When multiple threads share the same client handle, only one thread at a time can make a RPC request. The other threads must wait until the outstanding request is complete.

However, when multiple threads make RPC requests using unique client handles, the requests are carried out concurrently. The following diagram illustrates a possible timing of a multithreaded client implementation consisting of two client threads using different client handles.

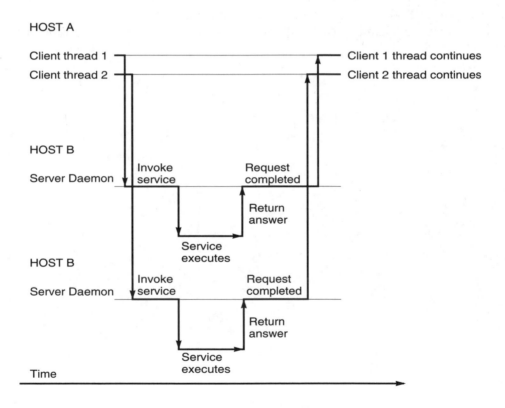

Figure A-1   Two Client Threads Using Different Client Handles (Realtime)

Code Example A-3 shows the implementation of an `rstat` program with a multithreaded client and single-threaded servers. The client program creates a thread for each host. Each thread creates its own client handle and makes various RPC calls to a specified host. Because each client thread uses its own handle to make the RPC calls, the threads can carry out the RPC calls concurrently.

You can compile and run this program with:

```
% cc -D_REENTRANT -o example example.c -lnsl -lrpcsvc -lthread
% example host1 host2 host3...
```

Code Example A-3   RPC `rstat` Program With Multithreaded Client

```
/* @(#)rstat.c2.3 88/11/30 4.0 RPCSRC */
/*
 * Simple program that prints the status of a remote host, in a
 * format similar to that used by the 'w' command.
 */

#include <thread.h>
#include <synch.h>
#include <stdio.h>
#include <sys/param.h>
#include <rpc/rpc.h>
#include <rpcsvc/rstat.h>
#include <errno.h>

mutex_t tty;          /* control of tty for printf's */
cond_t cv_finish;
int count = 0;
int nthreads = 0;

main(argc, argv)
    int argc;
    char **argv;
{
    int i;
    thread_t tid;
    void *do_rstat();

    if (argc < 2) {
```

Code Example A-3   RPC rstat Program With Multithreaded Client (Continued)

```
            fprintf(stderr, "usage: %s \"host\" [...]\n", argv[0]);
            exit(1);
    }

    mutex_lock(&tty);

    for (i = 1; i < argc; i++) {
        if (thr_create(NULL, 0, do_rstat, argv[i], 0, &tid) != 0) {
            fprintf(stderr, "thr_create failed: %d\n", i);
            exit(1);
        } else
            fprintf(stderr, "tid: %d\n", tid);
    }
nthreads = argc - 1;
    while (count < nthreads) {
        printf("argc = %d, count = %d\n", nthreads, count);
        cond_wait(&cv_finish, &tty);

    }

    exit(0);
}

bool_t rstatproc_stats();

void *
do_rstat(host)
    char *host;
{
    CLIENT *rstat_clnt;
    statstime host_stat;
    bool_t rval;
    struct tm *tmp_time;
    struct tm host_time;
    struct tm host_uptime;
    char days_buf[16];
    char hours_buf[16];

    mutex_lock(&tty);
    printf("%s: starting\n", host);
    mutex_unlock(&tty);

    /* client handle to rstat */
```

Code Example A-3   RPC rstat *Program With Multithreaded Client (Continued)*

```
rstat_clnt = clnt_create(host, RSTATPROG, RSTATVERS_TIME,
                    "udp");
if (rstat_clnt == NULL) {
    mutex_lock(&tty);       /* get control of tty */
    clnt_pcreateerror(host);
    count++;
    cond_signal(&cv_finish);
    mutex_unlock(&tty);/* release control of tty */

    thr_exit(0);

}

rval = rstatproc_stats(NULL, &host_stat, rstat_clnt);
if (!rval) {
    mutex_lock(&tty);/* get control of tty */
    clnt_perror(rstat_clnt, host);
    count++;
    cond_signal(&cv_finish);
    mutex_unlock(&tty);/* release control of tty */

    thr_exit(0);

}

tmp_time = localtime_r(&host_stat.curtime.tv_sec, &host_time);

host_stat.curtime.tv_sec -= host_stat.boottime.tv_sec;

tmp_time = gmtime_r(&host_stat.curtime.tv_sec, &host_uptime);

if (host_uptime.tm_yday != 0)
    sprintf(days_buf, "%d day%s, ", host_uptime.tm_yday,
    (host_uptime.tm_yday > 1) ? "s" : "");
else
    days_buf[0] = '\0';

if (host_uptime.tm_hour != 0)
    sprintf(hours_buf, "%2d:%02d,",
        host_uptime.tm_hour, host_uptime.tm_min);

else if (host_uptime.tm_min != 0)
    sprintf(hours_buf, "%2d mins,", host_uptime.tm_min);
```

Code Example A-3   RPC rstat *Program With Multithreaded Client (Continued)*

```
    else

        hours_buf[0] = '\0';

    mutex_lock(&tty);/* get control of tty */
    printf("%s: ", host);
    printf(" %2d:%02d%cm up %s%s load average: %.2f %.2f %.2f\n",
        (host_time.tm_hour > 12)  ? host_time.tm_hour - 12

        : host_time.tm_hour,
        host_time.tm_min,
        (host_time.tm_hour >= 12) ? 'p'
        : 'a',
        days_buf,
        hours_buf,
        (double)host_stat.avenrun[0]/FSCALE,
        (double)host_stat.avenrun[1]/FSCALE,
        (double)host_stat.avenrun[2]/FSCALE);
    count++;
    cond_signal(&cv_finish);
    mutex_unlock(&tty);/* release control of tty */
    clnt_destroy(rstat_clnt);

    sleep(10);
    thr_exit(0);
}

/*
Client side implementation of MT rstat program
*/

/* Default timeout can be changed using clnt_control() */
static struct timeval TIMEOUT = { 25, 0 };

bool_t
rstatproc_stats(argp, clnt_resp, clnt)
    void *argp;
    statstime *clnt_resp;
    CLIENT *clnt;
{

    memset((char *)clnt_resp, 0, sizeof (statstime));
    if (clnt_call(clnt, RSTATPROC_STATS,
```

Code Example A-3   RPC rstat *Program With Multithreaded Client (Continued)*

```
        (xdrproc_t) xdr_void, (caddr_t) argp,
        (xdrproc_t) xdr_statstime, (caddr_t) clnt_resp,
        TIMEOUT) != RPC_SUCCESS) {
        return (FALSE);

    }
    return (TRUE);
}
```

Window System Server

A networked window system server tries to handle each client application as independently as possible. Each application should get a fair share of the machine resources, and any blocking on I/O should affect only the connection that caused it.

You could assure that each application gets a fair share of machine resources by allocating a bound thread for each client application. While this would work, it is wasteful since more than a small subset of the clients are rarely active at any one time.

Allocating an LWP for each connection ties up large amounts of kernel resources basically for waiting. On a busy desktop, this can be several dozen LWPs. (A window system server designed to run with a single-level threads model would have different considerations about kernel resources and could be designed quite differently.)

The code shown in Code Example A-4 takes a different approach. It allocates two unbound threads for each client connection, one to process display requests and one to write out results.

This approach allows further input to be processed while the results are being sent, yet it maintains strict serialization within the connection. A single control thread looks for requests on the network. The relationship between threads is shown in Figure A-2.

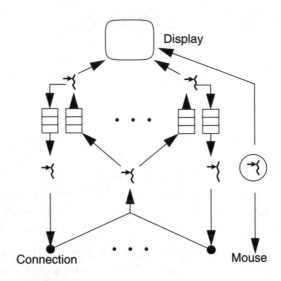

Figure A-2   Window Server Threads

With this arrangement, an LWP is used for the control thread and whatever threads happen to be active concurrently. The threads synchronize with queues. Each queue has its own mutex lock to maintain serialization, and a condition variable to inform waiting threads when something is placed on the queue. A bound thread processes mouse events to provide a quick response to inputs.

Code Example A-4   Window Server

```
main ()
{
    /* set up server and listen port */
    for(;;) {
        poll(&fds, nfds, 0);
        for (i = 0; i < nfds; i++) {
            if (fds[i].revents & POLLIN)
                checkfd(fds[i].fd)
        }
    }
```

Code Example A-4   Window Server (Continued)

```
}

checkfd (int fd)
{
    struct connection *connp;

    if (fd == listenfd) {
        /* new connection request */
        connp = create_new_connection();
        (void)thread_create (NULL, NULL, svc_requests, connp,
                        THR_DETACHED, NULL);
        (void) thread_create (NULL, NULL, send_replies, connp,
                        THR_DETACHED, NULL);
    } else {
        requestp = new_msg();
        requestp->len =
            t_rcv (fd, requestp->data, BUFSZ, &flags);
        connp = find_connection (fd);
        put_q (connp->input_q, requestp);
    }
}

send_replies (struct connection *connp)
{
    struct msg *replyp;

    while (1) {
        replyp = get_q (connp->output_q);
        t_snd (connp->fd, replyp->data, replyp->len, &flags);
    }
}

svc_requests (struct connection *connp)
{
    struct msg *requestp, *replyp;

    while (1) {
        requestp = get_q (connp->input_q);
        replyp = do_request (requestp);
        if (replyp)
            put_q (connp->output_q, replyp);
    }
}
```

Code Example A-4   Window Server (Continued)

```
put_q (struct queue *qp, struct msg *msgp)
{
    mutex_lock (&qp->lock);
    if (list_empty (qp->list))
        cond_signal (&qp->notempty_cond);
    add_to_tail (msgp, &qp->list);
    mutex_unlock (&qp->lock);
}


struct msg *
get_q struct queue *qp)
{
    struct msg *msgp;

    mutex_lock (&qp->lock);
    while (list_empty (qp->list))
        cond_wait (&qp->notempty_cond, &qp->lock);
    msgp = get_from_head (&qp->list);
    mutex_unlock (&qp->lock);
    return (msgp);
}
```

MT Safety Levels: Library Interfaces

Table B-1 lists the interfaces from Section 3 of the *man Pages(3): Library Routines* belonging to one of the *safe* categories. If an interface from Section 3 (not including the Source Compatibility library) is not in this table, it is probably unsafe. (See "MT Interface Safety Levels" on page 95 for explanations of the safety categories.)

Table B-1 MT Safety Levels of Library Interfaces

Interface (Man Page)	Category
_tolower (conv(3C))	MT-Safe with exceptions
_toupper (conv(3C))	MT-Safe with exceptions
a64l (a64l(3C))	MT-Safe
abort (abort(3C))	Safe
abs (abs(3C))	MT-Safe
acos (trig(3M))	MT-Safe
acosh (hyperbolic(3M))	MT-Safe
addseverity (addseverity(3C))	Safe
alloca (malloc(3C))	Safe
ascftime (strftime(3C))	Unsafe
asin (trig(3M))	MT-Safe
asinh (hyperbolic(3M))	MT-Safe
assert (assert(3X))	Safe
atan2 (trig(3M))	MT-Safe
atan (trig(3M))	MT-Safe
atanh (hyperbolic(3M))	MT-Safe
atexit (atexit(3C))	Safe
atof (strtod(3C))	MT-Safe
atoi (strtol(3C))	MT-Safe
atol (strtol(3C))	MT-Safe
atoll (strtol(3C))	MT-Safe
bessel (bessel(3M))	MT-Safe
bindtextdomain (gettext(3I))	Safe with exceptions
bsearch (bsearch(3C))	Safe
calloc (malloc(3C))	Safe

Table B-1   MT Safety Levels of Library Interfaces (Continued)

Interface (Man Page)	Category
calloc (malloc(3X))	Safe
calloc (mapmalloc(3X))	Safe
catclose (catopen(3C))	MT-Safe
catgets (catgets(3C))	MT-Safe
catopen (catopen(3C))	MT-Safe
cbrt (sqrt(3M))	MT-Safe
ceil (floor(3M))	MT-Safe
cfgetispeed (termios(3))	MT-Safe
cfgetospeed (termios(3))	MT-Safe
cfree (mapmalloc(3X))	Safe
cfsetispeed (termios(3))	MT-Safe
cfsetospeed (termios(3))	MT-Safe
cftime (strftime(3C))	Unsafe
clearerr (ferror(3S))	MT-Safe
clock (clock(3C))	MT-Safe
closedir (directory(3C))	Safe
closelog (syslog(3))	Safe
conv (conv(3C))	MT-Safe with exceptions
cos (trig(3M))	MT-Safe
cosh (hyperbolic(3M))	MT-Safe
crypt (crypt(3C))	Safe
csetcol (cset(3I))	MT-Safe with exceptions
cset (cset(3I))	MT-Safe with exceptions
csetlen (cset(3I))	MT-Safe with exceptions
csetno (cset(3I))	MT-Safe with exceptions
ctermid (ctermid(3S))	Unsafe
ctype (ctype(3C))	MT-Safe with exceptions
cuserid (cuserid(3S))	MT-Safe
decimal_to_quadruple (decimal_to_floating(3))	MT-Safe
decimal_to_single (decimal_to_floating(3))	MT-Safe
dgettext (gettext(3I))	Safe with exceptions
directory (directory(3C))	Safe
div (div(3C))	MT-Safe
dlclose (dlclose(3X))	MT-Safe
dlerror (dlerror(3X))	MT-Safe

Table B-1   MT Safety Levels of Library Interfaces (Continued)

Interface (Man Page)	Category
dlopen (dlopen(3X))	MT-Safe
dlsym (dlsym(3X))	MT-Safe
double_to_decimal (floating_to_decimal(3))	MT-Safe
drand48 (drand48(3C))	Safe
econvert (econvert(3))	MT-Safe
encrypt (crypt(3C))	Unsafe
erand48 (drand48(3C))	Safe
erfc (erf(3M))	MT-Safe
erf (erf(3M))	MT-Safe
euccol (euclen(3I))	Safe
euclen (euclen(3I))	Safe
eucscol (euclen(3I))	Safe
exit (exit(3C))	Safe
exp (exp(3M))	MT-Safe
extended_to_decimal (floating_to_decimal(3))	Mt-safe
fabs (ieee_functions(3M))	MT-Safe
fattach (fattach(3C))	MT-Safe
fclose (fclose(3S))	MT-Safe
fconvert (econvert(3))	MT-Safe
fdopen (fopen(3S))	MT-Safe
feof (ferror(3S))	MT-Safe
ferror (ferror(3S))	MT-Safe
fflush (fclose(3S))	MT-Safe
ffs (ffs(3C))	MT-Safe
fgetc (getc(3S))	MT-Safe
fgetpos (fsetpos(3C))	MT-Safe
fgets (gets(3S))	MT-Safe
fgetwc (getwc(3I))	MT-Safe
fgetws (getws(3I))	MT-Safe
fileno (ferror(3S))	MT-Safe
file_to_decimal (string_to_decimal(3))	MT-Safe
finite (isnan(3C))	MT-Safe
floor (floor(3M))	MT-Safe
fmod (ieee_functions(3M))	MT-Safe

Table B-1 MT Safety Levels of Library Interfaces (Continued)

Interface (Man Page)	Category
fmtmsg (fmtmsg(3C))	Safe
fopen (fopen(3S))	MT-Safe
fpclass (isnan(3C))	MT-Safe
fpgetmask (fpgetround(3C))	MT-Safe
fpgetround (fpgetround(3C))	MT-Safe
fpgetsticky (fpgetround(3C))	MT-Safe
fprintf (printf(3S))	MT-Safe, Async-Safe
fpsetmask (fpgetround(3C))	MT-Safe
fpsetround (fpgetround(3C))	MT-Safe
fpsetsticky (fpgetround(3C))	MT-Safe
fputc (putc(3S))	MT-Safe
fputs (puts(3S))	MT-Safe
fputwc (putwc(3I))	MT-Safe
fputws (putws(3I))	MT-Safe
fread (fread(3S))	MT-Safe
free (malloc(3C))	Safe
free (malloc(3X))	Safe
free (mapmalloc(3X))	Safe
freopen (fopen(3S))	MT-Safe
frexp (frexp(3C))	MT-Safe
fscanf (scanf(3S))	MT-Safe
fseek (fseek(3S))	MT-Safe
fsetpos (fsetpos(3C))	MT-Safe
ftell (fseek(3S))	MT-Safe
ftok (stdipc(3C))	MT-Safe
ftruncate (truncate(3C))	MT-Safe
ftw (ftw(3C))	Safe
func_to_decimal (string_to_decimal(3))	MT-Safe
fwrite (fread(3S))	MT-Safe
gconvert (econvert(3))	MT-Safe
getc (getc(3S))	MT-Safe
getchar (getc(3S))	MT-Safe
getchar_unlocked (getc(3S))	Unsafe
getc_unlocked (getc(3S))	Unsafe
getcwd (getcwd(3C))	Safe
getenv (getenv(3C))	Safe

Table B-1   MT Safety Levels of Library Interfaces (Continued)

Interface (Man Page)	Category
getlogin (getlogin(3C))	Unsafe
getmntany (getmntent(3C))	Safe
getmntent (getmntent(3C))	Safe
getpw (getpw(3C))	Safe
gets (gets(3S))	MT-Safe
getsubopt (getsubopt(3C))	MT-Safe
gettext (gettext(3I))	Safe with exceptions
gettimeofday (gettimeofday(3C))	MT-Safe
gettxt (gettxt(3C))	Safe with exceptions
getvfsany (getvfsent(3C))	Safe
getvfsent (getvfsent(3C))	Safe
getvfsfile (getvfsent(3C))	Safe
getvfsspec (getvfsent(3C))	Safe
getwc (getwc(3I))	MT-Safe
getwchar (getwc(3I))	MT-Safe
getw (getc(3S))	MT-Safe
getwidth (getwidth(3I))	MT-Safe with exceptions
getws (getws(3I))	MT-Safe
grantpt (grantpt(3C))	Safe
gsignal (ssignal(3C))	Unsafe
hasmntopt (getmntent(3C))	Safe
hcreate (hsearch(3C))	Safe
hdestroy (hsearch(3C))	Safe
hsearch (hsearch(3C))	Safe
hyperbolic (hyperbolic(3M))	MT-Safe
hypot (hypot(3M))	MT-Safe
ieee_functions (ieee_functions(3M))	MT-Safe
ieee_test (ieee_test(3M))	MT-Safe
isalnum (ctype(3C))	MT-Safe with exceptions
isalpha (ctype(3C))	MT-Safe with exceptions
isascii (ctype(3C))	MT-Safe with exceptions
isastream (isastream(3C))	MT-Safe
iscntrl (ctype(3C))	MT-Safe with exceptions
isdigit (ctype(3C))	MT-Safe with exceptions
isenglish (wctype(3I))	MT-Safe with exceptions
isgraph (ctype(3C))	MT-Safe with exceptions
isideogram (wctype(3I))	MT-Safe with exceptions

Table B-1   MT Safety Levels of Library Interfaces (Continued)

Interface (Man Page)	Category
islower (ctype(3C))	MT-Safe with exceptions
isnand (isnan(3C))	MT-Safe
isnan (ieee_functions(3M))	MT-Safe
isnan (isnan(3C))	MT-Safe
isnanf (isnan(3C))	MT-Safe
isnumber (wctype(3I))	MT-Safe with exceptions
isphonogram (wctype(3I))	MT-Safe with exceptions
isprint (ctype(3C))	MT-Safe with exceptions
ispunct (ctype(3C))	MT-Safe with exceptions
isspace (ctype(3C))	MT-Safe with exceptions
isspecial (wctype(3I))	MT-Safe with exceptions
isupper (ctype(3C))	MT-Safe with exceptions
iswalnum (wctype(3I))	MT-Safe with exceptions
iswalpha (wctype(3I))	MT-Safe with exceptions
iswascii (wctype(3I))	MT-Safe with exceptions
iswcntrl (wctype(3I))	MT-Safe with exceptions
iswdigit (wctype(3I))	MT-Safe with exceptions
iswgraph (wctype(3I))	MT-Safe with exceptions
iswlower (wctype(3I))	MT-Safe with exceptions
iswprint (wctype(3I))	MT-Safe with exceptions
iswpunct (wctype(3I))	MT-Safe with exceptions
iswspace (wctype(3I))	MT-Safe with exceptions
iswupper (wctype(3I))	MT-Safe with exceptions
iswxdigit (wctype(3I))	MT-Safe with exceptions
isxdigit (ctype(3C))	MT-Safe with exceptions
jrand48 (drand48(3C))	Safe
j0 (bessel(3M))	MT-Safe
j1 (bessel(3M))	MT-Safe
jn (bessel(3M))	MT-Safe
jrand48 (drand48(3C))	Safe
l64a (a64l(3C))	MT-Safe
labs (abs(3C))	MT-Safe
lckpwdf (lckpwdf(3C))	MT-Safe
lcong48 (drand48(3C))	Safe
ldexp (frexp(3C))	MT-Safe
ldiv (div(3C))	MT-Safe
lfind (lsearch(3C))	Safe

Table B-1 MT Safety Levels of Library Interfaces (Continued)

Interface (Man Page)	Category
llabs (abs(3C))	MT-Safe
lldiv (div(3C))	MT-Safe
lltostr (strtol(3C))	MT-Safe
localeconv (localeconv(3C))	Safe with exceptions
lockf (lockf(3C))	MT-Safe
log (exp(3M))	MT-Safe
log10 (exp(3M))	MT-Safe
logb (frexp(3C))	MT-Safe
logb (ieee_test(3M))	MT-Safe
lrand48 (drand48(3C))	Safe
lsearch (lsearch(3C))	Safe
madvise (madvise(3))	MT-Safe
major (makedev(3C))	MT-Safe
makecontext (makecontext(3C))	MT-Safe
makedev (makedev(3C))	MT-Safe
mallinfo (malloc(3X))	Safe
malloc (malloc(3C))	Safe
malloc (malloc(3X))	Safe
mallopt (malloc(3X))	Safe
mapmalloc (mapmalloc(3X))	Safe
matherr (matherr(3M))	MT-Safe
mbchar (mbchar(3C))	MT-Safe with exceptions
mblen (mbchar(3C))	MT-Safe with exceptions
mbstowcs (mbstring(3C))	MT-Safe with exceptions
mbstring (mbstring(3C))	MT-Safe with exceptions
mbtowc (mbchar(3C))	MT-Safe with exceptions
memalign (malloc(3C))	Safe
memccpy (memory(3C))	MT-Safe
memchr (memory(3C))	MT-Safe
memcmp (memory(3C))	MT-Safe
memcntl (memcntl(3))	MT-Safe
memcpy (memory(3C))	MT-Safe
memmove (memory(3C))	MT-Safe
memory (memory(3C))	MT-Safe
memset (memory(3C))	MT-Safe
minor (makedev(3C))	MT-Safe
mkfifo (mkfifo(3C))	MT-Safe

Table B-1   MT Safety Levels of Library Interfaces (Continued)

Interface (Man Page)	Category
mktemp (mktemp(3C))	Safe
mlockall (mlockall(3C))	MT-Safe
mlock (mlock(3C))	MT-Safe
modf (frexp(3C))	MT-Safe
modff (frexp(3C))	MT-Safe
monitor (monitor(3C))	Safe
mrand48 (drand48(3C))	Safe
msync (msync(3C))	MT-Safe
munlockall (mlockall(3C))	MT-Safe
munlock (mlock(3C))	MT-Safe
nextafter (frexp(3C))	MT-Safe
nextafter (ieee_functions(3M))	MT-Safe
nftw (ftw(3C))	Safe with exceptions
nl_langinfo (nl_langinfo(3C))	Safe with exceptions
nlist (nlist(3E))	Safe
nrand48 (drand48(3C))	Safe
offsetof (offsetof(3C))	MT-Safe
opendir (directory(3C))	Safe
openlog (syslog(3))	Safe
perror (perror(3C))	MT-Safe
pow (exp(3M))	MT-Safe
printf (printf(3S))	MT-Safe, Async-Safe
psiginfo (psignal(3C))	Safe
psignal (psignal(3C))	Safe
ptsname (ptsname(3C))	Safe
putc (putc(3S))	MT-Safe
putchar (putc(3S))	MT-Safe
putenv (putenv(3C))	Safe
putmntent (getmntent(3C))	Safe
puts (puts(3S))	MT-Safe
putwc (putwc(3I))	MT-Safe
putwchar (putwc(3I))	MT-Safe
putw (putc(3S))	MT-Safe
putws (putws(3I))	MT-Safe
qsort (qsort(3C))	Safe
quadruple_to_decimal (floating_to_decimal(3))	MT-Safe

Table B-1   MT Safety Levels of Library Interfaces (Continued)

Interface (Man Page)	Category
raise (raise(3C))	MT-Safe
readdir (directory(3C))	Unsafe
realloc (malloc(3C))	Safe
realloc (malloc(3X))	Safe
realpath (realpath(3C))	MT-Safe
remainder (ieee_functions(3M))	MT-Safe
remove (remove(3C))	MT-Safe
rewinddir (directory(3C))	Safe
rewind (fseek(3S))	MT-Safe
scalb (frexp(3C))	MT-Safe
scalb (ieee_test(3M))	MT-Safe
scanf (scanf(3S))	MT-Safe
seconvert (econvert(3))	MT-Safe
seed48 (drand48(3C))	Safe
seekdir (directory(3C))	Safe
select (select(3C))	MT-Safe
setbuf (setbuf(3S))	MT-Safe
setkey (crypt(3C))	Safe
setlocale (setlocale(3C))	Safe with exceptions
setlogmask (syslog(3))	Safe
settimeofday (gettimeofday(3C))	MT-Safe
setvbuf (setbuf(3S))	MT-Safe
sfconvert (econvert(3))	MT-Safe
sgconvert (econvert(3))	MT-Safe
sigaddset (sigsetops(3C))	MT-Safe
sigdelset (sigsetops(3C))	MT-Safe
sigemptyset (sigsetops(3C))	MT-Safe
sigfillset (sigsetops(3C))	MT-Safe
sigismember (sigsetops(3C))	MT-Safe
significand (ieee_test(3M))	MT-Safe
sigsetops (sigsetops(3C))	MT-Safe
sin (trig(3M))	MT-Safe
single_to_decimal (floating_to_decimal(3))	MT-Safe
sinh (hyperbolic(3M))	MT-Safe
sleep (sleep(3C))	Safe
sprintf (printf(3S))	MT-Safe

Table B-1 MT Safety Levels of Library Interfaces (Continued)

Interface (Man Page)	Category
sqrt (sqrt(3M))	MT-Safe
srand48 (drand48(3C))	Safe
sscanf (scanf(3S))	MT-Safe
ssignal (ssignal(3C))	Unsafe
strcasecmp (string(3C))	MT-Safe
strcat (string(3C))	MT-Safe
strchr (string(3C))	MT-Safe
strcmp (string(3C))	MT-Safe
strcoll (strcoll(3C))	Safe with exceptions
strcpy (string(3C))	MT-Safe
strcspn (string(3C))	MT-Safe
strdup (string(3C))	MT-Safe
strerror (strerror(3C))	Safe
strftime (strftime(3C))	Unsafe
string (string(3C))	MT-Safe
string_to_decimal (string_to_decimal(3))	MT-Safe
strlen (string(3C))	MT-Safe
strncasecmp (string(3C))	MT-Safe
strncat (string(3C))	MT-Safe
strncmp (string(3C))	MT-Safe
strncpy (string(3C))	MT-Safe
strpbrk (string(3C))	MT-Safe
strrchr (string(3C))	MT-Safe
strsignal (strsignal(3C))	Safe
strspn (string(3C))	MT-Safe
strstr (string(3C))	MT-Safe
strtod (strtod(3C))	MT-Safe
strtok (string(3C))	Unsafe
strtol (strtol(3C))	MT-Safe
strtoll (strtol(3C))	MT-Safe
strtoul (strtol(3C))	MT-Safe
strtoull (strtol(3C))	MT-Safe
strxfrm (strxfrm(3C))	Safe with exceptions
swab (swab(3C))	MT-Safe
swapcontext (makecontext(3C))	MT-Safe
sysconf (sysconf(3C))	Safe

Table B-1   MT Safety Levels of Library Interfaces (Continued)

Interface (Man Page)	Category
syslog (syslog(3))	Safe
system (system(3S))	MT-Safe
t_accept (t_accept(3N))	MT-Safe
t_alloc (t_alloc(3N))	MT-Safe
t_bind (t_bind(3N))	MT-Safe
t_close (t_close(3N))	MT-Safe
t_connect (t_connect(3N))	MT-Safe
t_error (t_error(3N))	MT-Safe
t_free (t_free(3N))	MT-Safe
t_getinfo (t_getinfo(3N))	MT-Safe
t_getstate (t_getstate(3N))	MT-Safe
t_listen (t_listen(3N))	MT-Safe
t_look (t_look(3N))	MT-Safe
t_open (t_open(3N))	MT-Safe
t_optmgmt (t_optmgmt(3N))	MT-Safe
t_rcvconnect (t_rcvconnect(3N))	MT-Safe
t_rcvdis (t_rcvdis(3N))	MT-Safe
t_rcv (t_rcv(3N))	MT-Safe
t_rcvrel (t_rcvrel(3N))	MT-Safe
t_rcvudata (t_rcvudata(3N))	MT-Safe
t_rcvuderr (t_rcvuderr(3N))	MT-Safe
t_snddis (t_snddis(3N))	MT-Safe
t_snd (t_snd(3N))	MT-Safe
t_sndrel (t_sndrel(3N))	MT-Safe
t_sndudata (t_sndudata(3N))	MT-Safe
t_sync (t_sync(3N))	MT-Safe
t_unbind (t_unbind(3N))	MT-Safe
tan (trig(3M))	MT-Safe
tanh (hyperbolic(3M))	MT-Safe
tcdrain (termios(3))	MT-Safe
tcflow (termios(3))	MT-Safe
tcflush (termios(3))	MT-Safe
tcgetattr (termios(3))	MT-Safe
tcgetpgrp (termios(3))	MT-Safe
tcgetsid (termios(3))	MT-Safe
tcsendbreak (termios(3))	MT-Safe
tcsetattr (termios(3))	MT-Safe

Table B-1 MT Safety Levels of Library Interfaces (Continued)

Interface (Man Page)	Category
tcsetpgrp (tcsetpgrp(3C))	MT-Safe
tcsetpgrp (termios(3))	MT-Safe
tdelete (tsearch(3C))	Safe
tempnam (tmpnam(3S))	Safe
telldir (directory(3C))	Safe
termios (termios(3))	MT-Safe
textdomain (gettext(3I))	Safe with exceptions
tfind (tsearch(3C))	Safe
tmpfile (tmpfile(3S))	Safe
tmpnam (tmpnam(3S))	Unsafe
toascii (conv(3C))	MT-Safe with exceptions
tolower (conv(3C))	MT-Safe with exceptions
toupper (conv(3C))	MT-Safe with exceptions
towlower (wconv(3I))	MT-Safe with exceptions
towupper (wconv(3I))	MT-Safe with exceptions
trig (trig(3M))	MT-Safe
truncate (truncate(3C))	MT-Safe
tsearch (tsearch(3C))	Safe
ttyslot (ttyslot(3C))	Safe
twalk (tsearch(3C))	Safe
ulckpwdf (lckpwdf(3C))	MT-Safe
ulltostr (strtol(3C))	MT-Safe
ungetc (ungetc(3S))	MT-Safe
ungetwc (ungetwc(3I))	MT-Safe
unlockpt (unlockpt(3C))	Safe
unordered (isnan(3C))	MT-Safe
valloc (malloc(3C))	Safe
vfprintf (vprintf(3S))	MT-Safe
vprintf (vprintf(3S))	Async-Safe
vsprintf (vprintf(3S))	Async-Safe
vsyslog (vsyslog(3))	Safe
watof (wstod(3I))	MT-Safe
watoi (wstol(3I))	MT-Safe
watol (wstol(3I))	MT-Safe
watoll (wstol(3I))	MT-Safe
wconv (wconv(3I))	MT-Safe with exceptions
wcsetno (cset(3I))	MT-Safe with exceptions

Table B-1   MT Safety Levels of Library Interfaces (Continued)

Interface (Man Page)	Category
wcstombs (mbstring(3C))	MT-Safe with exceptions
wctomb (mbchar(3C))	MT-Safe with exceptions
wctype (wctype(3I))	MT-Safe with exceptions
windex (wstring(3I))	MT-Safe
wrindex (wstring(3I))	MT-Safe
wscat (wstring(3I))	MT-Safe
wschr (wstring(3I))	MT-Safe
wscmp (wstring(3I))	MT-Safe
wscol (wstring(3I))	MT-Safe
wscoll (wscoll(3I))	Safe with exceptions
wscpy (wstring(3I))	MT-Safe
wscspn (wstring(3I))	MT-Safe
wsdup (wstring(3I))	MT-Safe
wslen (wstring(3I))	MT-Safe
wsncat (wstring(3I))	MT-Safe
wsncmp (wstring(3I))	MT-Safe
wsncpy (wstring(3I))	MT-Safe
wspbrk (wstring(3I))	MT-Safe
wsprintf (wsprintf(3I))	MT-Safe
wsrchr (wstring(3I))	MT-Safe
wsscanf (wsscanf(3I))	MT-Safe
wsspn (wstring(3I))	MT-Safe
wstod (wstod(3I))	MT-Safe
wstok (wstring(3I))	MT-Safe
wstol (wstol(3I))	MT-Safe
wstring (wstring(3I))	MT-Safe
wsxfrm (wsxfrm(3I))	Safe with exceptions
y0 (bessel(3M))	MT-Safe
y1 (bessel(3M))	MT-Safe
yn (bessel(3M))	MT-Safe

B

Multithreaded Programming Guide

Index

F

finding
    minimum stack size, 30
    thread concurrency level, 31
    thread priority, 32
fine-grained locking, 109
flockfile(3S), 91
fork cleanup handler, 74
fork(2), 46, 50, 73, 74
fork1(2), 73, 74
FORTRAN, 102
funlockfile(3S), 91

G

getc(3S), 91
getc_unlocked(3S), 91
gethostbyname(3N), 107
gethostbyname_r(3N), 107
getrusage(3B), 75
global
    data, 109
    memory, 101
    state, 109
    thread scheduling, 8
    variables, 23, 24, 101, 105, 106

H

heap, malloc(3C) storage from, 20

I

I/O
    asynchronous, 88
    nonsequential, 90
    standard, 91
    synchronous, 88
inheriting priority, 12
interrupt, 79
interval timer, 75, 115
invariants, 55, 110

J

joining threads, 18

K

kernel context switching, 5
kernel-level threads, 5
keys
    bind value to key, 22
    destructor function, 21
    get specific key, 22
    global into private, 24
    storing value of, 21, 22
    for TSD, 21
kill(2), 79, 82

L

-lc, 100
ld, 100
libC, 97
libc, 97, 99, 100
libdl_stubs, 97
libintl, 97, 99
libm, 97, 99
libmalloc, 97, 99
libmapmalloc, 97, 99
libnsl, 97, 99, 100
library
    C routines, 105
    threads, 6, 11 to 72, 99
libresolv, 97
libsocket, 97
libthread, 5, 6, 11, 99, 100
libw, 97, 99
libX11, 97
lightweight processes, 7, 8, 76 to 78, 81
    adding an LWP, 28
    creation, 8
    debugging, 102
    defined, 2
    independence, 7
    multiplexing, 7
    no time-slicing of threads, 34

TLI, 97, 100

tools
    adb, 102
    dbx, 102
    debugger, 9, 102
    lock_lint, 41
    truss, 9

total store order, 119

trap, 79

truss, 9

TS, *See* timeshare scheduling class

TSD, *See* thread-specific data

U

unbound threads, 76
    alternate signal stacks, 79
    caching, 113
    concurrency, 31, 114
    defined, 2, 8
    disadvantage, 8
    floating, 8
    mixing with bound threads, 8
    priorities, 32, 76
    reasons not to bind, 113, 115
    and scheduling, 76, 77, 78
    and THR_NEW_LWP, 13
    and thr_setconcurrency(3T), 114
    and thr_setprio(3T), 76, 78

UNIX, 1, 5, 9, 79, 88, 90, 106

user space, 5

user-level threads, 2, 5

USYNC_PROCESS, 37, 46, 58, 65, 70, 114

USYNC_THREAD, 37, 46, 58, 65, 70

V

V operation, 63

variables
    condition, 35, 45 to 61, 72
    global, 101
    local, 101
    primitive, 36

verhogen, 63

vfork(2), 74

W

write(2), 90

X

XDR, 97